Personal & Social Skills

Activities Featuring Kagan Structures

Lisa Mitchell
Sarah Walas Teed
Lynsy Oswald

Kagan

Kagan Publishing
981 Calle Amanecer
San Clemente, CA 92673
800.933.2667
www.KaganOnline.com

ISBN: 978-1-933445-54-0

Table of Contents

Table of Contents

Section 2: Emotional Intelligence..........53

Table of Contents

Section 3: Character Education..........79

Section 4: Answer Key..........117

Table of Structures

Table of Structures

Introduction

Dear Educators,

We hope you find these lessons to be as useful and as engaging as we do. By teaching social skills, your students will be better classmates and friends. In so many ways, you as the teacher set the climate and culture in your classroom. Addressing social and emotional needs is the foundation for developing successful and happy people. Thank you for teaching our future leaders how to be kind to themselves and others. As educators, we don't always get to see the payoff of what we do, but trust and keep faith that we are making the world a better place by investing in the lives of children. YOU make a difference! We understand how hard your job is each day, but we are thankful for you. Keep up the great work!

We would like to thank the Moline-Coal Valley School District for supporting Kagan Cooperative Learning. The students in Moline-Coal Valley are blessed to have administrators who value staff professional development and have invested in the importance of cooperative learning. The students are also very fortunate to have teachers who want their students to be social and engaged while learning. We would also like to thank the staff at Hamilton Elementary School for being awesome coworkers and friends. We feel very thankful to work with the best!

We appreciate Miguel Kagan for his guidance and review of our manuscripts. Thank you Alex Core for making the book come alive with your book designs and cover. Thank you also to Becky Herrington for managing the publication. We enjoyed working with you! Thank you to Ginny Harvey for copy editing, and Erin Kant, your illustrations brought our visions to life! We are so impressed with the entire Kagan team and grateful to have had the chance to work with all of you on this book!

Enjoy!
Lisa, Sarah, and Lynsy

About the Authors

Lisa Mitchell is currently an Instructional Coach for the Moline-Coal Valley School District. She began her career 30-plus years ago as a special education teacher working with students with severe social and emotional disorders. She moved into regular education in 2000 and has taught 1st, 2nd, 3rd, and 4th grade. Lisa started using Kagan Structures in her classroom to help promote positive learning and engagement in her students. She serves as a Kagan Coach for her building. Lisa is married to Paul, who is a Middle School Social Studies teacher. They both love to follow the Red Sox with their son Derek and spend time with their other son Damon and his family, Wendy and granddaughter Elena. In her free time, Lisa loves to read, work out, and travel to warm, sunny places.

Sarah Walas Teed is a school counselor for the Moline-Coal Valley School District. Sarah is a building Kagan Coach and likes using Kagan Structures in her lessons because of the natural ways they build social skills and engagement. These lessons are what you will find her teaching in her classroom. Sarah wants to be an advocate for all her students and help everyone feel welcomed, appreciated, and successful in their learning. Sarah loves to spend time with her husband Jace (also a school counselor), son Cylus, daughter Seneca, and her parents, siblings, and her husband's family. Her family is also very excited to welcome a new baby on the way! Sarah loves Jesus and wants to give Him the glory in all she does.

Lynsy Oswald is an Assistant Principal for the Moline-Coal Valley School District. She is also a Curriculum and Assessment Specialist for Kids at the Core. Lynsy is currently a Kagan Coach and a Kagan School Trainer in Moline. She is passionate about engaging students and helping them grow as learners and as people. Lynsy lives with her husband Rob, her step-daughter Lily, and her two crazy dogs Bella and Riley. In her free time she loves to travel, walk her dogs, play golf, cheer on Lily, spend time with her niece Maddie and her nephews Blake and Owen, and be with her family. She is thankful for her parents' unconditional love and support.

Social Skills Development

School Appropriate Conversation Topics

Jot Thoughts

Purpose

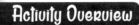

- To teach students appropriate conversation topics for school

Group Size

- Teams

Materials

- 10–20 sticky notes or small writing paper pieces per team
- 1 writing utensil per student
- 1 class timer (optional)
- 1 School Appropriate Conversation Topics Brainstorming Mat (optional)
- 1 School Appropriate Conversation Topics Sorting Mat (optional)

Preteaching

- Using a T-chart, give examples of things that are okay and not okay to talk about at school.
- Explain why some things are not appropriate for school.

Activity Overview

Students each have multiple slips of paper. Teammates "cover the table," writing ideas about school appropriate conversation topics on their slips of paper.

Activity Steps

1. The teacher names a topic such as school appropriate conversation topics, sets a time limit, and provides Think Time. (E.g., *"Think about how many fun ideas you can talk about with peers at school."*)

2. Students write and announce as many ideas as they can in the allotted time, one idea per sticky note or slip of paper. You can also use the optional Brainstorming Mat. Students place their sticky notes on the mat as they come up with ideas.

3. After generating ideas, students may sort their ideas into categories. The Sorting Mat is designed for sorting ideas into categories. Students label the top of each box for each category.

Note: You can have teams share ideas to compile a classroom list, or teams can share their ideas with other teams.

Structure Alternatives

- *RallyRobin*
- *Talking Chips*

School Appropriate Conversation Topics

Jot Thoughts Brainstorming Mat

Directions: Copy this mat for each team. Write the topic in the center of the mat. Students place sticky notes on the mat as they brainstorm ideas.

____

Topic

School Appropriate Conversation Topics

Jot Thoughts Sorting Mat

Directions: Copy this mat for each team. Students use it to sort ideas they brainstormed.

______________________	______________________
______________________	______________________

Conflict Resolution

Mix-Pair-Share

Purpose

- To increase the peace throughout the school
- To enable students to know how to problem solve

Group Size

- Pairs

Materials

- 1 set of Conflict Resolution cards per class

Preteaching

- Review your expectations about how conflicts should be solved within your classroom. Give examples.
- Teach how respect, responsibility, and safety are all part of conflict resolution.

Activity Overview

The class "mixes" until the teacher calls, "Pair." The teacher asks students questions about conflict resolution. Students share with their partner and then find a new partner to discuss or answer the teacher's question about conflict resolution.

Activity Steps

1. The students mix around the room.
2. The teacher calls, *"Pair."*
3. Students pair up with the person closest to them and give a high five. Students who haven't found a partner raise their hands to quickly find each other.
4. The teacher asks a question such as, *"What is a safe way to solve a conflict?"*, and gives students Think Time.
5. Students share with their partners using Timed Pair Share.

Structure Alternatives

- *Fan-N-Pick*
- *Numbered Heads Together*
- *Talking Chips*

Conflict Resolution

Mix-Pair-Share Cards

Directions: Cut out each card along the dotted lines. In pairs, students take turns responding to the question or statement.

1 Conflict Resolution

What are some reasons you and your friends have conflicts?

Mix-Pair-Share

2 Conflict Resolution

How do you like to be treated when someone is upset with you?

Mix-Pair-Share

3 Conflict Resolution

What is a safe way to solve a conflict?

Mix-Pair-Share

4 Conflict Resolution

Conflict happens! How can you keep a conflict from becoming a big issue?

Mix-Pair-Share

5 Conflict Resolution

Explain how you could stay calm during a conflict.

Mix-Pair-Share

6 Conflict Resolution

You are having a disagreement with a teacher at school. How can you show respect while discussing the problem?

Mix-Pair-Share

Conflict Resolution

Mix-Pair-Share Cards

Directions: Cut out each card along the dotted lines. In pairs, students take turns responding to the question or statement.

7 Conflict Resolution

Who do you know that is good at solving conflicts safely and respectfully? What does that person do?

Mix-Pair-Share

8 Conflict Resolution

You are having a disagreement with a friend at school. What could you do to make the problem smaller?

Mix-Pair-Share

9 Conflict Resolution

Describe a time in which you handled a conflict peacefully. What did you do? What did you say? What did you NOT do?

Mix-Pair-Share

10 Conflict Resolution

What are safe methods you use to calm down when you are angry or upset? Name at least two.

Mix-Pair-Share

11 Conflict Resolution

What do most kids argue about at our school? How could this be avoided?

Mix-Pair-Share

12 Conflict Resolution

How can you show respect to someone in a conflict?

Mix-Pair-Share

Conflict Resolution

Mix-Pair-Share Blank Template

Directions: Use these blank cards to create your own Mix-Pair-Share Conflict Resolution cards.

Conflict Resolution

Mix-Pair-Share

Conflict Resolution

Mix-Pair-Share

Conflict Resolution

Mix-Pair-Share

Conflict Resolution

Mix-Pair-Share

Conflict Resolution

Mix-Pair-Share

Conflict Resolution

Mix-Pair-Share

Dealing with Teasing

Find Someone Who

Purpose

- **To teach students how to respond when someone is mean**

Group Size

- Pairs

Materials

- 1 Dealing with Teasing Worksheet per student
- 1 writing utensil per student

Preteaching

- Teach respectful and responsible behavior. Everyone has had someone be mean to them. It happens sometimes. It is important to know respectful and responsible ways to respond to teasing.
- Teach strategies to students so they know how to respond after being teased. Some ideas might be to walk away, ignore, find an adult, speak up and disagree, or use an I-Message.
- Teach students when to make a report to an adult and when to handle the problem alone.

Activity Overview

Students play Find Someone Who to respond to questions or statements about dealing with teasing.

Activity Steps

1. Students mix in the class, keeping a hand raised until they find a partner who is not a teammate.
2. In pairs, Partner A asks a question from the Dealing with Teasing Worksheet; Partner B responds. Partner A records the answer on his or her own Dealing with Teasing Worksheet and expresses appreciation.
3. Partner B checks and initials the answer.
4. Partner B asks a question about dealing with teasing. Partner A responds. Partner B records the answer on his or her own Dealing with Teasing Worksheet and expresses appreciation.
5. Partner A checks and initials the answer.
6. Partners shake hands, part, and raise a hand again as they search for a new partner.
7. Students repeat Steps 1–6 until their Dealing with Teasing Worksheets are complete.
8. When their worksheets are complete, students sit down; seated students may be approached by others as a resource.
9. In teams, students compare answers using RoundRobin. If there is a disagreement or uncertainty, they raise four hands to ask a team question.

Dealing with Teasing

Find Someone Who Worksheet

Directions: Pair up and take turns answering one question or statement. Don't forget to get your partner's initials.

Name ______________________________

1 Dealing with Teasing

If someone hurts your feelings, what plan do you have on how to respond?

____

____

______________________ Initials

2 Dealing with Teasing

Describe how you would stay calm after being teased by someone.

____

____

______________________ Initials

3 Dealing with Teasing

What would you say in a respectful way if you saw someone teasing someone else? ______________________________

____

______________________ Initials

4 Dealing with Teasing

Explain when to report a problem to the teacher.

____

____

______________________ Initials

5 Dealing with Teasing

Describe what responsible and respectful students do after being teased. ______________________________

____

______________________ Initials

6 Dealing with Teasing

How can you handle a teasing problem by yourself?

____

____

______________________ Initials

7 Dealing with Teasing

If someone calls you a rude name, what should you say in response?

____

____

______________________ Initials

Dealing with Teasing

Find Someone Who Blank Template

Directions: Use this blank worksheet to create your own Find Someone Who dealing with teasing questions.

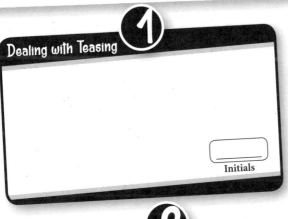

Name ______________________________

1 Dealing with Teasing

Initials

2 Dealing with Teasing

Initials

3 Dealing with Teasing

Initials

4 Dealing with Teasing

Initials

5 Dealing with Teasing

Initials

6 Dealing with Teasing

Initials

7 Dealing with Teasing

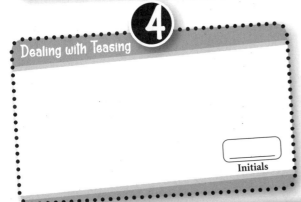

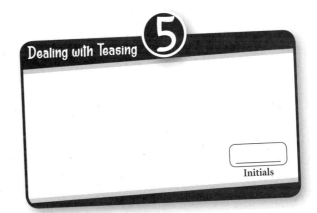

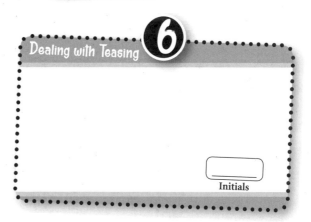

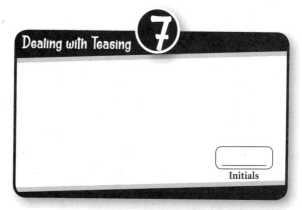

Initials

Dealing with Rumors and Gossip

Jot Thoughts

Purpose

- **To teach students how to respond appropriately if someone is talking about them**

Group Size

- Teams

Materials

- 10–20 sticky notes or small writing paper pieces per team
- 1 writing utensil per student
- 1 class timer (optional)
- 1 Dealing with Rumors and Gossip Brainstorming Mat (optional)
- 1 Dealing with Rumors and Gossip Sorting Mat (optional)

Preteaching

- Teach the meaning of the words gossip and rumors.
- Explain about how gossip and rumors are harmful to a respectful class environment.
- Give students some ideas on how to respond if someone is talking about them behind their back. Explain how some responses make the problem bigger and how respectful ideas might make the problem smaller.

Activity Overview

Students each have multiple slips of paper. Teammates "cover the table," writing ideas about dealing with rumors and gossip on their slips of paper.

Activity Steps

1. The teacher names a topic such as how to deal with rumors and gossip, sets a time limit, and provides Think Time. (E.g., *"Think about respectful ways you could respond to rumors or gossip."*)

2. Students write and announce as many ideas as they can in the allotted time, one idea per sticky note or slip of paper. You can use the optional Brainstorming Mat. Students place their sticky notes on the mat as they come up with ideas.

3. After generating ideas, students may sort their ideas into categories. The Sorting Mat is designed for sorting ideas into categories. Students label the top of each box for each category.

Note: You can have teams share ideas to compile a classroom list, or teams can share their ideas with other teams.

Structure Alternatives

- *RallyRobin*
- *Talking Chips*

Dealing with Rumors and Gossip

Jot Thoughts Brainstorming Mat

Directions: Copy this mat for each team. Write the topic in the center of the mat. Students place sticky notes on the mat as they brainstorm ideas.

____

Topic

Dealing with Rumors and Gossip

Jot Thoughts Sorting Mat

Directions: Copy this mat for each team. Students use it to sort ideas they brainstormed.

______________________	______________________
______________________	______________________

Diversity Appreciation

Find Someone Who

Purpose

- To promote classbuilding
- To recognize and appreciate that we are all different

Group Size

- Pairs

Materials

- 1 Diversity Appreciation Worksheet per student
- 1 writing utensil per student

Preteaching

- Teach students the meaning of the word "diversity." Explain that it is a good thing; that we are all different.

Activity Overview

Students play Find Someone Who to respond to questions or statements about diversity appreciation.

Activity Steps

1. Students mix in the class, keeping a hand raised until they find a new partner who is not a teammate.
2. In pairs, Partner A asks a question from the Diversity Appreciation Worksheet; Partner B responds. Partner A records the answer on his or her own Diversity Appreciation Worksheet and expresses appreciation.
3. Partner B checks and initials the answer.
4. Partner B asks a question about diversity. Partner A responds. Partner B records the answer on his or her own Diversity Appreciation Worksheet and expresses appreciation.
5. Partner A checks and initials the answer.
6. Partners shake hands, part, and raise a hand again as they search for a new partner.
7. Students repeat Steps 1–6 until their Diversity Appreciation Worksheets are complete.
8. When their worksheets are complete, students sit down; seated students may be approached by others as a resource.
9. In teams, students compare answers using RoundRobin. If there is a disagreement or uncertainty, they raise four hands to ask a team question.

Diversity Appreciation

Find Someone Who Worksheet

Name ______________________

Directions: Pair up and take turns answering one question. Don't forget to get your partner's initials.

Have you been to another country? Which one? ___ Initials	Can you speak more than one language? What other language? ___ Initials	Do you know your family heritage? What is it? ___ Initials
Does your family have a unique holiday tradition? What do you do? ___ Initials	Do you have a special talent or interest? What is it? ___ Initials	Have you lived somewhere other than this city? Where? ___ Initials
Do you have a food that is special to your family? What is it? ___ Initials	Do you have a special dream or goal for the future? What is it? ___ Initials	What is your understanding of diversity? ___ Initials

Diversity Appreciation

Find Someone Who Blank Template

Name ______________________________

Directions: Use this blank worksheet to create your own Find Someone Who diversity appreciation questions.

Initials	Initials	Initials
Initials	Initials	Initials
Initials	Initials	Initials

Getting Along

Timed Pair Share

Purpose

- To increase the peace throughout the school
- To enable students to know how to problem solve

Group Size

- Pairs

Materials

- 1 set of Getting Along cards per class or pair
- 1 class timer

Preteaching

- Explain the I-Message format. *"I feel ______ when ______ because ______."*
- Explain the basic apology format. *"I'm sorry because ______. Next time I will ______."*

Activity Overview

In pairs, students take turns sharing their responses to questions or statements about getting along.

Activity Steps

1. The teacher either reads a Getting Along card or Partner A draws a card and reads it aloud to his or her partner. The teacher states that each student will have 20 seconds to share, and then provides Think Time for students to think about how they will respond.
2. In pairs, Partner A shares and Partner B listens.
3. Partner B responds with praise.
4. Partners switch roles: Partner B responds to the question, and then Partner A praises Partner B for his or her response.

Structure Alternatives

- *Mix-Pair-Share*
- *Fan-N-Pick*
- *RoundRobin*
- *Talking Chips*

Getting Along

Timed Pair Share Cards

Directions: Cut out cards along the dotted lines. Students share answers to the questions using Timed Pair Share.

1 Getting Along

At recess, a student in your class comes up to you and says another student is talking about you behind your back. How could you handle this problem respectfully?

Timed Pair Share

2 Getting Along

Someone in your class is bothering you during silent work time. How could you quietly ask him or her to stop?

Timed Pair Share

3 Getting Along

Someone in your class continuously gives you dirty looks. What is one thing you can do to stop this problem?

Timed Pair Share

4 Getting Along

Your shoulder partner is goofing around during a math activity. What words would you use to ask him or her to start participating?

Timed Pair Share

5 Getting Along

You accidently bump someone in line. What words should you say to let him or her know it was an accident?

Timed Pair Share

6 Getting Along

You say something mean to one of your friends. You feel guilty and upset about your mistake. Give an example of an apology you could say to your friend.

Timed Pair Share

7 Getting Along

At recess, you ask to play basketball and someone says no. What is another activity you could do instead?

Timed Pair Share

8 Getting Along

You are upset that someone said, *"Your shoes are ugly."* Give an example of an I-Message you could say in response.

Timed Pair Share

Getting Along

Timed Pair Share Cards

Directions: Cut out cards along the dotted lines. Students share answers to the questions using Timed Pair Share.

9 Getting Along

Who in the school can give you help if you don't know how to handle a problem with a friend?

Timed Pair Share

10 Getting Along

You've asked someone nicely several times to stop calling you stupid. What is the next step in solving this problem?

Timed Pair Share

11 Getting Along

There is a rumor going around that someone wants to fight you. What can you say to make it clear you do not want to fight?

Timed Pair Share

12 Getting Along

Someone is talking about something inappropriate at lunch. What is an appropriate conversation topic you could bring up?

Timed Pair Share

13 Getting Along

During an activity, your shoulder partner calls you, "*dumb.*" Give an example of an I-message you could say in response.

Timed Pair Share

14 Getting Along

Your face partner tells you that when you tap your pencil, it really bothers him. What should you say to him in response?

Timed Pair Share

15 Getting Along

You are annoyed that someone in your class keeps making jokes about chicken. What is an I-Message you could say to ask him or her to stop?

Timed Pair Share

16 Getting Along

Someone in your class says something really mean about one of your friends. Give an example of an I-Message you could say in response.

Timed Pair Share

Getting Along

Timed Pair Share Blank Template

Directions: Use these blank cards to create your own Timed Pair Share Getting Along cards.

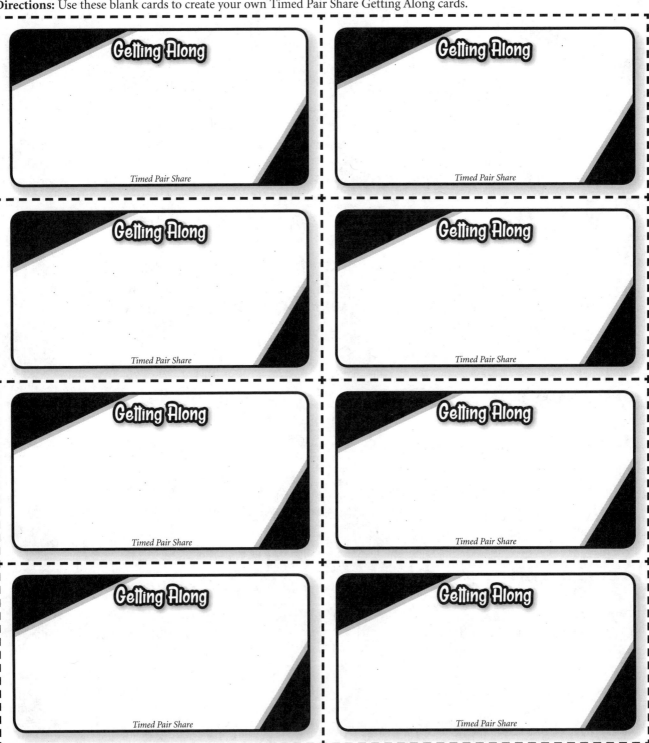

Getting Along

Timed Pair Share

Getting Along

Timed Pair Share

Getting Along

Timed Pair Share

Getting Along

Timed Pair Share

Getting Along

Timed Pair Share

Getting Along

Timed Pair Share

Getting Along

Timed Pair Share

Getting Along

Timed Pair Share

Getting Along

Showdown

Purpose

- To increase the peace throughout the school
- To enable students to know how to problem solve

Group Size

- Teams

Materials

- 1 set of Getting Along cards per team
- 1 "Bigger" and 1 "Smaller" response card per student

Preteaching

- Tell students it is normal that sometimes students have problems getting along with each other. But at school, it is expected that we solve the problem respectfully (nicely).
- Explaining our actions (or how we handle a situation) makes the problem either bigger or smaller.

Activity Overview

Teams play Showdown to respond to questions about getting along. Students select either a "Bigger" or "Smaller" response card, indicating whether the behavior will make the problem bigger or smaller.

Activity Steps

1. The teacher selects one student on each team to be the Showdown Captain for the first round.
2. The Showdown Captain draws the top card, reads the statement about getting along to the team, and provides Think Time.
3. Students independently decide if the actions make the problem bigger or smaller.
4. When finished, teammates signal they are ready by holding their selected response card against their chest.
5. The Showdown Captain calls, *"Showdown."*
6. Teammates show their response card and discuss why they chose "Bigger" or "Smaller."
7. The Showdown Captain leads the checking.
8. If correct, the team celebrates; if not, teammates tutor and then celebrate. If consensus can't be reached with the students, all four hands are raised and the teacher consults.
9. The person on the left of the Showdown Captain becomes the Showdown Captain for the next round.

Note: For younger students, the teacher can be the Showdown Captain and lead the group or class in Showdown.

Getting Along

Showdown Response Cards

Directions: Cut out each card along the dotted lines. Give each student one "Bigger" and one "Smaller" response card to play Showdown.

Getting Along

Bigger

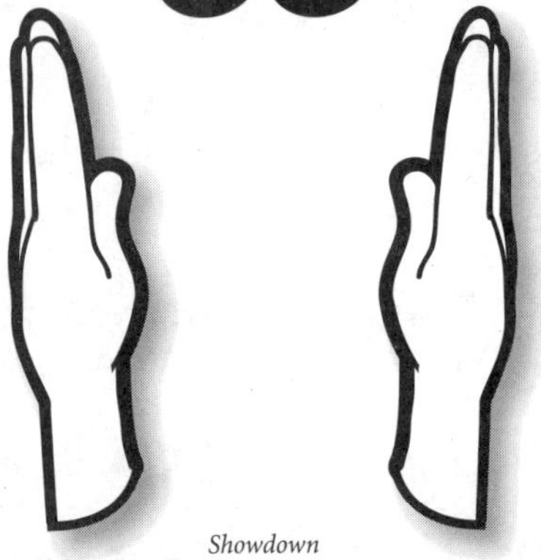

Showdown

Getting Along

Bigger

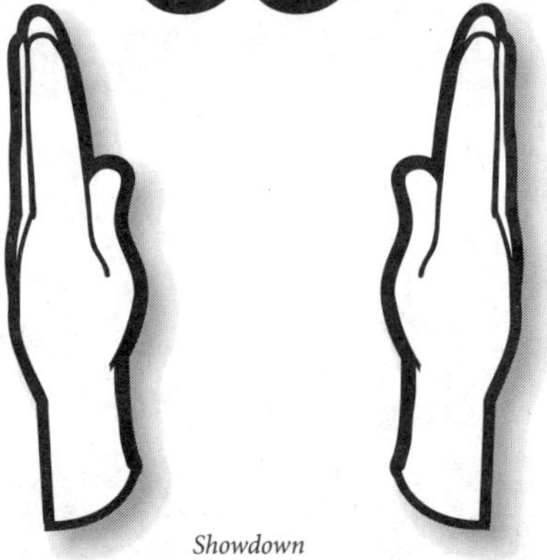

Showdown

Getting Along

Smaller

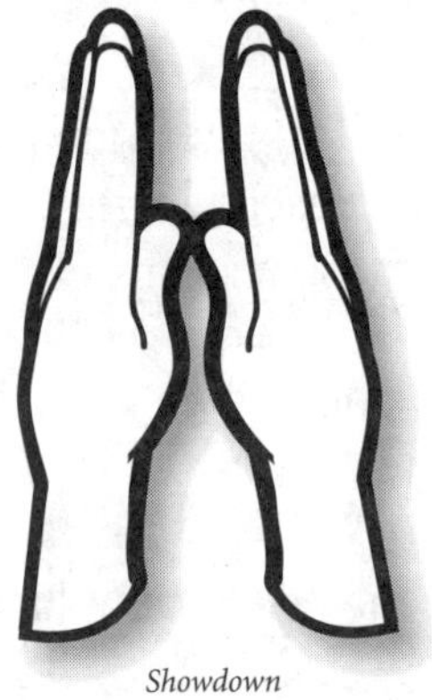

Showdown

Getting Along

Smaller

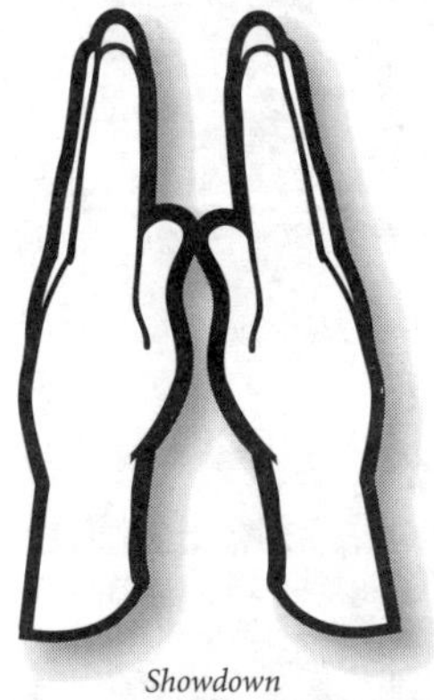

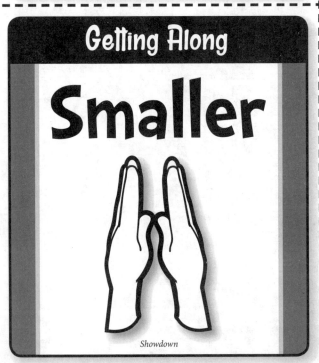

Showdown

Getting Along

Showdown Cards

Directions: Cut out each card along the dotted lines. Give each team a set of cards to play Showdown.

1 Getting Along

Stevie accidently bumped into Jennifer. Stevie immediately says, *"Excuse me."*

Showdown

2 Getting Along

Billy gives Joe a mean look. Joe just looks away.

Showdown

3 Getting Along

Stephanie feels crowded in line so she pushes the student ahead of her.

Showdown

4 Getting Along

Jaquon's shoulder partner tells him that it is annoying how he taps his pencil. Jaquon taps it louder and harder trying to bother someone else.

Showdown

5 Getting Along

Laura picks her nose. The kids in her class see and say, *"Gross!"* Laura stops picking her nose and asks to go wash her hands.

Showdown

6 Getting Along

César called José dumb during math. José says, *"I feel mad when you call me dumb because that's rude. Please stop!"*

Showdown

7 Getting Along

At recess, kids won't let James play basketball. Instead of crying, James just runs over to play hopscotch instead.

Showdown

8 Getting Along

Ashton feels lonely because no one in his group is talking to him. He starts making dog noises to get his group to look at him.

Showdown

9 Getting Along

Laura makes a mistake during calendar time. Sarah points and laughs at her loudly.

Showdown

10 Getting Along

Tom laughed when Mikayla made a mistake. Mikayla said, *"I feel mad when you laugh at me because that is mean. Please stop."*

Showdown

Getting Along

Showdown Cards

Directions: Cut out each card along the dotted lines. Give each team a set of cards to play Showdown.

11 Getting Along

Daniel drops his crayons. Everyone around him helps him pick them up.

Showdown

12 Getting Along

Trenton feels lonely at recess because no one is playing with him. He stands by the wall and cries.

Showdown

13 Getting Along

Lance gets out during dodge ball in P.E. He feels disappointed and wants to cry, but instead just says, *"Oh Well!"* and walks to the side and sits down.

Showdown

14 Getting Along

Giselle is mad at Kianna so she sticks out her tongue at her.

Showdown

15 Getting Along

Abby is trying to be funny for her friends so at indoor recess she starts throwing play dough.

Showdown

16 Getting Along

Alex said something mean to Stevie. Now Alex feels guilty, so he says, *"I'm sorry that I said I don't like you, Stevie. I do like you!"*

Showdown

17 Getting Along

There is a **REALLY** long line at the drinking fountain. José stands with his hands to himself and waits patiently.

Showdown

18 Getting Along

The teacher on duty at recess blows the whistle and signals for Jane to come to her. Instead of coming over, Jane laughs and runs away.

Showdown

19 Getting Along

Logan makes a mistake during math. His shoulder partner says, *"Good try, but try again!"*

Showdown

20 Getting Along

Stephanie feels mad because her best friend said her drawing was bad. Stephanie says, *"I feel mad when you say my drawing is bad because I tried my best. Please don't say that."*

Showdown

Getting to Know You

Mix-Pair-Share

Purpose

- **To promote classbuilding**

Group Size

- Pairs

Materials

- 1 set of Getting to Know You cards per class

Preteaching

- Remind students how respectful partners act.

Activity Overview

The class "mixes" until the teacher calls, "Pair." *The teacher asks students questions helping them get to know each other. Students share with their partner and then find a new partner to discuss or answer the teacher's question, getting to know each other.*

Activity Steps

1. The students mix around the room.
2. The teacher calls, *"Pair."*
3. Students pair up with the person closest to them and give a high five. Students who haven't found a partner raise their hands to quickly find each other.
4. The teacher asks a question such as, *"What do you like to eat for breakfast?"*, and gives students Think Time.
5. Students share with their partners using Timed Pair Share.

Structure Alternatives

- *Fan-N-Pick*
- *Numbered Heads Together*
- *Talking Chips*

Getting to Know You

Mix-Pair-Share Cards

Directions: Cut out each card along the dotted lines. In pairs, students take turns responding to the question.

1 Getting to Know You

If you could go anywhere for a vacation, where would it be?

Mix-Pair-Share

2 Getting to Know You

What super power would you like to have? What would you do with your power?

Mix-Pair-Share

3 Getting to Know You

What do you like to eat for breakfast? Describe a delicious breakfast.

Mix-Pair-Share

4 Getting to Know You

What are your talents?

Mix-Pair-Share

5 Getting to Know You

Do you have any pets? What kind?

Mix-Pair-Share

6 Getting to Know You

What TV shows do you like to watch?

Mix-Pair-Share

7 Getting to Know You

What would you buy if you won lots of money?

Mix-Pair-Share

8 Getting to Know You

What is your favorite school lunch?

Mix-Pair-Share

Getting to Know You

Mix-Pair-Share Cards

Directions: Cut out each card along the dotted lines. In pairs, students take turns responding to the question.

9 — Getting to Know You

What kind of books do you like to read?

Mix-Pair-Share

10 — Getting to Know You

Who is in your family? List the members of your family.

Mix-Pair-Share

11 — Getting to Know You

What do you do for fun?

Mix-Pair-Share

12 — Getting to Know You

What is your favorite restaurant? What do you like to order?

Mix-Pair-Share

13 — Getting to Know You

What is a sport you enjoy? Do you prefer to watch or play? Why?

Mix-Pair-Share

14 — Getting to Know You

What are two things that make you happy?

Mix-Pair-Share

15 — Getting to Know You

If you have brothers and sisters, what are their names?

Mix-Pair-Share

16 — Getting to Know You

What is your favorite movie? Why do you like it so much?

Mix-Pair-Share

Getting to Know You

Mix-Pair-Share Blank Template

Directions: Use these blank cards to create your own Mix-Pair-Share Getting to Know You cards.

Getting to Know You

Mix-Pair-Share

Getting to Know You

Mix-Pair-Share

Getting to Know You

Mix-Pair-Share

Getting to Know You

Mix-Pair-Share

Getting to Know You

Mix-Pair-Share

Getting to Know You

Mix-Pair-Share

Getting to Know You

Mix-Pair-Share

Getting to Know You

Mix-Pair-Share

Getting to Know You

Three-Step Interview

Purpose

- **To help students with communication and social skills**
- **To learn more about their teammates and classmates**

Group Size

- Pairs and Teams

Materials

- 1 Getting To Know You Worksheet per student
- 1 writing utensil per student
- 1 class timer

Preteaching

- Discuss appropriate things to ask your teammate/classmate.

Activity Overview

In pairs, students interview each other with questions about getting to know you and then share with teammates what they learned.

Activity Steps

1. The teacher provides the interview topic, *"getting to know you,"* and sets a time limit.
2. In pairs, Student A interviews Student B using the questions from the Getting to Know You Worksheet. Student B talks while Student A listens and records.
3. Pairs switch roles. Student B interviews Student A. Student A talks while Student B listens and/or coaches and records.
4. RoundRobin—pairs pair up to form teams of four. Each student takes turns sharing with the team what he or she learned about his or her partner from the interview.

Structure Alternative
- *Timed Pair Share*

Getting to Know You

Three-Step Interview Worksheet

Directions: Take turns interviewing your partner. Record your partner's answers and then share answers with your team.

Getting to Know You Interview Questions

★ Who do you live with? ____________________

★ Do you have any siblings? How many? ____________________

★ Do you have any pets? What kind? ____________________

★ What is your biggest fear? Why? ____________________

★ What is your biggest accomplishment so far? ____________________

★ What do you want to be when you grow up? Why? ____________________

★ What do you like to do for fun? ____________________

★ What is your favorite summer activity? ____________________

★ What is your favorite winter activity? ____________________

★ What is your favorite season? Why? ____________________

★ What is your favorite thing about school? Why? ____________________

Giving Compliments

Mix-Pair-Share

Purpose

- **To promote classbuilding**
- **To teach students how to say friendly words to each other**

Group Size

- Pairs

Materials

- 1 Set of Giving Compliments cards per class

Preteaching

- Teach students the word "compliment." Explain that compliments are a friendly way to promote each other.
- Model how to give appropriate compliments and body language when giving a compliment.

Activity Overview

The class "mixes" until the teacher calls, "Pair." The teacher asks students questions about giving compliments. Students share with their partner and then find a new partner to discuss or answer the teacher's question about giving compliments.

Activity Steps

1. The students mix around the room.
2. The teacher calls, *"Pair."*
3. Students pair up with the person closest to them and give a high five. Students who haven't found a partner raise their hands to quickly find each other.
4. The teacher asks a question such as, "*What is a compliment you could give a partner?*", and gives students Think Time.
5. Students share with their partners using Timed Pair Share.

Structure Alternative

Give students the sentence stems, "I like your…" *and* "You are…" *Then have the student do StandUp–HandUp–PairUp to find a partner. Both partners give each other a compliment (they can use the sentence stems) and then thank each other. Then students put their hands up to find another partner. This continues until the teacher calls time (usually 3–4 minutes).*

Giving Compliments

Mix-Pair-Share Cards

Directions: Cut out each card along the dotted lines. In pairs, students take turns responding to the question.

1 Giving Compliments

What is a compliment you could give a partner?

Mix-Pair-Share

2 Giving Compliments

How do you feel when you receive a compliment?

Mix-Pair-Share

3 Giving Compliments

What is one compliment you received that really made you feel good?

Mix-Pair-Share

4 Giving Compliments

When would be a good time to congratulate or praise someone?

Mix-Pair-Share

5 Giving Compliments

What is a compliment you could give someone based on his or her appearance?

Mix-Pair-Share

6 Giving Compliments

What is a compliment you could give someone based on his or her effort?

Mix-Pair-Share

7 Giving Compliments

Do you know someone who gives others a lot of compliments? How do people feel about him or her?

Mix-Pair-Share

8 Giving Compliments

If someone pays you a compliment should you say "thanks," return a compliment, or both?

Mix-Pair-Share

Hands and Feet to Self

Showdown

Purpose

- To increase the safety of all students in the building
- To teach or reteach students what is expected of their hands and feet while at school

Group Size

- Teams

Materials

- 1 set of Hands and Feet to Self cards per team
- 1 "OK!" and 1 "Not OK!" response card per student

Preteaching

- Teach the concept of personal space. Give examples of when personal space is very important within the school building.
- Teach line space. Demonstrate appropriate distance between students in a class line.

Activity Overview

Teams play Showdown to respond to questions about keeping their hands and feet to themselves. Students respond to each question with an "OK!" or a "Not OK!" response card.

Activity Steps

1. The teacher selects one student on each team to be the Showdown Captain for the first round.
2. The Showdown Captain draws the top card, reads the statement about keeping your hands and feet to yourself to the team, and provides Think Time.
3. Students independently decide if the behavior is "OK" or "Not OK."
4. When finished, teammates signal they are ready by holding their selected response card against their chest.
5. The Showdown Captain calls, *"Showdown."*
6. Teammates show their response card and discuss why they chose "OK!" or "Not OK!"
7. The Showdown Captain leads the checking.
8. If correct, the team celebrates; if not, teammates tutor and then they celebrate. If consensus can't be reached with the students, all four hands are raised and the teacher consults.
9. The person on the left of the Showdown Captain becomes the Showdown Captain for the next round.

Note: For younger students, the teacher can be the Showdown Captain and lead the group or class in Showdown.

Hands and Feet to Self

Showdown Response Cards

Directions: Cut out each card along the dotted lines. Give each student one "OK!" and one "Not OK!" response card to play Showdown.

Hands and Feet to Self

Showdown Cards

Directions: Cut out each card along the dotted lines. Give each team a set of cards to play Showdown.

1 Hands and Feet to Self

In the lunch line, Evan puts his hands on Steven's shoulders.

Showdown

2 Hands and Feet to Self

In the bathroom, Stephanie is careful not to bump into anyone.

Showdown

3 Hands and Feet to Self

José walks with his hands by his side in the hallway.

Showdown

4 Hands and Feet to Self

George is mad at Zoey but instead of hitting her, he uses his words to give an I-message. *"I feel mad when you take my crayons without asking. Please give my crayons back!"*

Showdown

5 Hands and Feet to Self

Sarah hits Lisa because Lisa gave her a mean look.

Showdown

6 Hands and Feet to Self

Maria tries to hug Esperanza in the hallway.

Showdown

7 Hands and Feet to Self

William keeps poking his pencil at Jesús' arm.

Showdown

8 Hands and Feet to Self

At the drinking fountain, Jace keeps his hands and feet to himself and doesn't squish the person in front of him.

Showdown

9 Hands and Feet to Self

Alan remembers to give line space when walking from his class to P.E.

Showdown

10 Hands and Feet to Self

While sitting on the carpet, Molly sits so close to Sonia that their legs touch.

Showdown

Hands and Feet to Self

Showdown Cards

Directions: Cut out each card along the dotted lines. Give each team a set of cards to play Showdown.

11 — Hands and Feet to Self

During an assembly, Addison makes sure she sits criss-cross and that her legs and hands don't touch anyone else.

Showdown

12 — Hands and Feet to Self

While walking in line, Kena makes sure she walks at the right speed so she doesn't step on anyone's shoes.

Showdown

13 — Hands and Feet to Self

At lunch, Cindy feels squished. She says to the person next to her, *"Could you please move over a little bit?"* The person moves right away.

Showdown

14 — Hands and Feet to Self

When sitting at a table with other students, Tom makes sure to not touch anyone else's materials or area.

Showdown

15 — Hands and Feet to Self

Todd feels squished in line so he pushes the person in front of him.

Showdown

16 — Hands and Feet to Self

At recess, Shayla tries to pick up Catalina to show how strong she is.

Showdown

17 — Hands and Feet to Self

Before school, Daniel keeps his backpack on his back and his hands and feet to himself while he waits to enter the building.

Showdown

18 — Hands and Feet to Self

Grant is mad at recess. He thinks about pushing Adele because she is mean, but instead of pushing, he walks away to play with someone else.

Showdown

19 — Hands and Feet to Self

Layla kicked her friend Anya under the table to get her attention.

Showdown

20 — Hands and Feet to Self

Sebastion put his hands over Kayla's eyes while they were walking in line.

Showdown

Sharing Ideas (Raising Hand)

RallyTable and Pairs Compare

Purpose

- To increase positive social behaviors in the classroom
- To teach or reteach students when to raise their hand and when to speak without permission

Group Size

- Pairs (RallyTable) and Teams (Pairs Compare)

Materials

- 1 Sharing Ideas Worksheet per pair
- 1 writing utensil per student

Preteaching

- Ask students why we have the rule to raise our hands.
- Review when students need to raise their hand and when they can speak without permission.

Activity Overview

In pairs, students take turns generating examples about sharing ideas. Together, students list examples in either the "Raise Hand" column or the "Just Talk" column. Pairs compare their answers with another pair.

Activity Steps

RallyTable:

1. The teacher announces the topic is *"sharing ideas at school"* and passes out the Sharing Ideas Worksheet to each pair. The teacher tells students that they will generate a list of examples of when it's appropriate to raise a hand under the "Raise Hand" column, and when to talk under the "Just Talk" column.
2. The teacher asks students to think about raising hands vs. just talking and provides Think Time.
3. The teacher announces which student will start the list.
4. Students write an idea in one column and the opposite idea in the other. (For example, raise hand during math lesson and just talk with partner.) Students pass the paper back and forth to each other after they have made a contribution. (Students may not pass the paper without making a contribution. They may not make more than one contribution at a time.)
5. The teacher calls time.

Pairs Compare:

6. Pairs pair to RoundRobin their answers. For each answer, the face partner in the other pair adds the answer to that pair's list or checks it off if they already had it.
7. As a team of four, they see if they can come up with additional ideas.

Structure Alternatives

- *Jot Thoughts*
- *Talking Chips*
- *AllRecord RoundRobin*

Sharing Ideas

RallyTable and Pairs Compare Worksheet

Directions: Take turns listing when to raise a hand or to just talk in the appropriate columns.

Raise Hand	Just Talk
Example: During math lesson **Example:** In hallway	**Example:** Partner work **Example:** Recess

Emotional Intelligence

Calming Down

Swap Talk

Purpose

- **To give students ideas on how to calm down when feeling upset**

Group Size

- Pairs

Materials

- 1 Calming Down card per student
- 1 writing utensil per student
- 1 class timer

Preteaching

- Give the students several appropriate strategies to use when needing to calm down.
- Share with students that everyone gets upset. It is okay to get upset. However, you need to know how to show your feelings appropriately.

Activity Overview

Students do multiple pairings, each time swapping cards. With each pairing, they each share information on the card they're holding as well as ask each other a question from the card.

Activity Steps

1. Students each receive a Calming Down card. They respond to how they can calm down when upset. They also write a question on the card about calming down.
2. With their completed cards in hand, students stand up, put a hand up, and pair up.
3. Partners take turns sharing the information on their cards and asking and responding to the question.
4. Students swap cards, thank their partner, and put a hand up to find a new partner.
5. With their new partners, students take turns sharing information on the card and asking the question. For example, *"One way Hollyn can calm down when she's upset is ..."*
6. The process is continued until the teacher calls, *"stop,"* or *"time is up."* With each new pairing, students have a new card with new information and a new question.

Structure Alternatives

- *Timed Pair Share*
- *RoundRobin*

Calming Down

Swap Talk Cards

Directions: Cut out each Calming Down card along the dotted lines. Each student receives a card and fills it out to play Swap Talk.

Name ______________________

★ What is one way you calm down when upset? ______________________

★ Question: ______________________

Name ______________________

★ What is one way you calm down when upset? ______________________

★ Question: ______________________

Feeling Annoyed

AllRecord Consensus

Purpose

- To teach kids it is okay to be annoyed
- To build relationships with teammates

Group Size

- Teams

Materials

- 1 Feeling Annoyed Recording Sheet per student
- 1 writing utensil per student
- 1 class timer

Preteaching

- Review what feeling annoyed means.
- Discuss with students that it is okay to be annoyed and the ways you can handle these feelings.

Activity Overview

In teams, students take turns stating a definition or example of feeling annoyed. If there is consensus, all teammates reword the idea on their sheets.

Activity Steps

1. The teacher may break down feeling annoyed into different sections such as feeling disappointed, feeling impatient, etc. The teacher then selects a student on each team to begin.
2. The selected teammate suggests the first description of how it feels to be annoyed or provides an example of when he or she felt annoyed.
3. Teammates put thumbs up, down, or sideways to indicate agreement, disagreement, or doubt.
4. If teammates agree, all students write the answer on their Feeling Annoyed Worksheets. If there is disagreement or doubt, the team discusses the answer until agreement is reached.
5. The process is continued: each student in turn suggests a new idea RoundRobin-style, the team reaches consensus, and then all teammates record the idea.

Structure Alternatives

- *RoundRobin*
- *AllRecord RoundRobin*

Feeling Annoyed

AllRecord Consensus Recording Sheet

Directions: After reaching consensus, all teammates record the idea on this worksheet.

Feeling Annoyed Recording Sheet

1. ______________________________

2. ______________________________

3. ______________________________

4. ______________________________

5. ______________________________

6. ______________________________

7. ______________________________

8. ______________________________

9. ______________________________

10. ______________________________

Feeling Mad

Jot Thoughts

Purpose

- **To teach students how to show and express mad feelings in a safe and appropriate way**

Group Size

- Teams

Materials

- 10–20 sticky notes or small writing paper pieces per team
- 1 writing utensil per student
- 1 class timer (optional)
- 1 Feeling Mad Brainstorming Mat (optional)
- 1 Feeling Mad Sorting Mat (optional)

Preteaching

- Tell students it is okay to be mad. Everyone gets mad. But we have to show our mad feelings in a safe and appropriate way.
- Teach the anger rule. It is okay to feel angry but don't hurt others, yourself, or property. Do talk about what is making you angry!
- Make a list of anger busters! Anger busters are safe ways to calm down.

Activity Overview

Students each have multiple slips of paper. Teammates "cover the table," writing ideas about feeling mad on their slips of paper.

Activity Steps

1. The teacher names a topic such as, *"feeling mad,"* sets a time limit, and provides Think Time. (E.g., *"In three minutes, come up with examples of things that make you feel mad and how can you calm down?")*

2. Students write and announce as many ideas as they can in the allotted time, one idea per sticky note or slip of paper. You can use the optional Brainstorming Mat. Students place their sticky notes on the mat as they come up with ideas.

3. After generating ideas, students may sort their ideas into categories. The Sorting Mat is designed for sorting ideas into categories. Students label the top of each box for each category.

Note: You can have teams share ideas to compile a classroom list, or teams can share their ideas with other teams.

Structure Alternatives

- *RallyRobin*
- *Talking Chips*

Feeling Mad

Jot Thoughts Brainstorming Mat

Directions: Copy this mat for each team. Write the topic in the center of the mat. Students place sticky notes on the mat as they brainstorm ideas.

____

Topic

Feeling Mad

Jot Thoughts Sorting Mat

Directions: Copy this mat for each team. Students use it to sort ideas they brainstormed.

Feeling Mad

Three-Step Interview

Purpose

- To teach students it is okay to be mad
- To learn more about each other's teammates and classmates

Group Size

- Pairs and Teams

Materials

- 1 Feeling Mad Worksheet per student
- 1 writing utensil per student
- 1 class timer

Preteaching

- Discuss appropriate ways to show you are mad.

Activity Overview

In pairs, students interview each other with questions about feeling mad and then share with teammates what they learned.

Activity Steps

1. The teacher provides the interview topic, *"feeling mad,"* and sets a time limit.
2. In pairs, Student A interviews Student B using the questions from the Feeling Mad Worksheet. Student B talks while Student A listens and records.
3. Pairs switch roles. Student B interviews Student A. Student A talks while Student B listens and/or coaches and records.
4. RoundRobin—pairs pair up to form teams of four. Each student takes turns sharing with the team what he or she learned about feeling mad from the interview.

Structure Alternative

- *Timed Pair Share*

Feeling Mad

Three-Step Interview Worksheet

Directions: Take turns interviewing your partner. Record your partner's answers and then share answers with your team.

Feeling Mad Interview Questions

1. What are some things that make you mad? ______________________
2. Why do some things make you mad? ______________________
3. What person calms you down when you are mad? ______________________
4. What thought could you have that will calm you down? ______________________
5. Where is a place you can go to calm down at school? ______________________
6. Why is it important to show you are mad safely? ______________________
7. What can happen if you do not show you are mad in a safe way? ______________________
8. Who does it hurt if you do not show you are mad in a safe way? ______________________
9. Describe an appropriate way to show you are mad. ______________________
10. Tell about a time you were mad and calmed down safely. ______________________
11. What happens to your body when you feel mad? ______________________
12. What are safe words you could use to tell someone you are mad? ______________________

Feeling Sad

Timed Pair Share

Purpose

- **To teach students how to recognize and express feeling sad safely and appropriately**

Group Size

- Pairs

Materials

- 1 set of Feeling Sad cards per class or pair
- 1 class timer

Preteaching

- Teach students it is okay to be sad. Everyone gets sad. Using a T-chart, explain to students that there are acceptable and not acceptable ways to act when sad.

Activity Overview

In pairs, students take turns sharing their responses to questions or statements about feeling sad.

Activity Steps

1. The teacher either reads a Feeling Sad card or Partner A draws a card and reads it aloud to his or her partner. The teacher states that each student will have 20 seconds to share, and then provides Think Time for students to think about how they will respond.
2. In pairs, Partner A shares and Partner B listens.
3. Partner B responds with praise.
4. Partners switch roles: Partner B responds to the question, and then Partner A praises Partner B for his or her response.

Structure Alternatives
- *Mix-Pair-Share*
- *Fan-N-Pick*
- *RoundRobin*
- *Talking Chips*

Feeling Sad

Timed Pair Share Cards

Directions: Cut out cards along the dotted lines. Students share answers to the questions using Timed Pair Share.

1 Feeling Sad

When do you feel sad? Why?

Timed Pair Share

2 Feeling Sad

When I'm sad, it is okay for me to _______.

Timed Pair Share

3 Feeling Sad

When I'm sad, it is not okay for me to _______.

Timed Pair Share

4 Feeling Sad

Who can you talk to if you are sad? What could you say?

Timed Pair Share

5 Feeling Sad

If you see that someone else is sad, what could you do or say to show you care?

Timed Pair Share

6 Feeling Sad

What helps you feel better if you are feeling sad?

Timed Pair Share

Feeling Disappointed

Swap Talk

Purpose

- **To let students know it is okay to feel disappointed and that everyone is disappointed at times**

Group Size

- Pairs

Materials

- 1 Feeling Disappointed card per student
- 1 writing utensil per student
- 1 class timer

Preteaching

- Teach students what it means to be "disappointed."
- Teach students appropriate ways to handle disappointment.

Activity Overview

Students do multiple pairings, each time swapping cards. With each pairing, they each share information on the card they're holding as well as ask each other a question from the card.

Activity Steps

1. Students each receive a Feeling Disappointed card. They respond to how they safely handled feeling disappointed. They also write a question on the card about feeling disappointed.
2. With their completed cards in hand, students stand up, put a hand up, and pair up.
3. Partners take turns sharing the information on their cards and asking and responding to the question.
4. Students swap cards, thank their partner, and put a hand up to find a new partner.
5. With their new partners, students take turns sharing information on the card and asking the question. For example, *"Wyatt safely handled his disappointment by…"*
6. The process is continued until the teacher calls, *"stop,"* or *"time is up."* With each new pairing, students have a new card with new information and a new question.

Structure Alternatives

- *Timed Pair Share*
- *RoundRobin*

Feeling Disappointed

Swap Talk Cards

Directions: Cut out each Feeling Disappointed card along the dotted lines. Each student receives a card and fills it out to play Swap Talk.

Name ______________________

★ **How did you safely handle your disappointment?** ______________________

____

____

____

____

★ **Question:** ______________________

____

____

____

Name ______________________

★ **How did you safely handle your disappointment?** ______________________

____

____

____

____

★ **Question:** ______________________

____

____

____

Feeling Lonely or Left Out

RallyRobin

Purpose

- To make sure all students understand how to safely express and show the feeling of being lonely
- To empower students who are feeling left out at school on how to handle this problem

Group Size

- Pairs

Preteaching

- Teach students that it is okay to be lonely! Everyone feels left out or lonely sometimes. When we are lonely, we have to show our lonely feelings in a safe and appropriate way. Briefly discuss what the students have witnessed that other students have done to handle being left out. Compare each behavior to see if it fixes the problem of being left out or makes it worse. Make sure to discuss topics from the list of behaviors that can make the lonely problem worse or ideas for making it better.

Activity Overview

In pairs, students take turns orally listing ideas about feeling lonely or left out.

Activity Steps

1. The teacher announces the topic, *"If I am feeling lonely or left out, I can…,"* and provides Think Time.
2. In pairs, partners take turns listing ideas about what they can do if they are feeling lonely or left out.
3. This back-and-forth verbal rally continues until the teacher calls time.

Discuss with the class if these behaviors make the problem better or worse.

- Physical aggression
- Pouting
- Whining
- Tattling
- Begging
- Being mean
- Back stabbing
- Playing a game by yourself
- Asking someone else to play
- Finding a way to be included
- Watching or cheering

Structure Alternatives

- *Jot Thoughts (write instead of talk)*
- *Talking Chips*

Feeling Scared

Timed Pair Share

Purpose

- **To teach students how to safely recognize and appropriately express the feeling of being scared**

Group Size

- Pairs

Materials

- 1 set of Feeling Scared cards per class or pair
- 1 class timer

Preteaching

- Teach students it is okay to be scared. Everyone gets scared!
- Using a T-chart, explain that there are ways that are okay and not okay to act when scared.

Activity Overview

In pairs, students take turns sharing their responses to questions about feeling scared.

Activity Steps

1. The teacher either reads a Feeling Scared card or Partner A draws a card and reads it aloud to his or her partner. The teacher states that each student will have 20 seconds to share, and then provides Think Time for students to think how they will respond.
2. In pairs, Partner A shares and Partner B listens.
3. Partner B responds with praise.
4. Partners switch roles: Partner B responds to the question, and then Partner A praises Partner B for his or her response.

Structure Alternatives
- *Mix-Pair-Share*
- *Fan-N-Pick*
- *RallyRobin*
- *Talking Chips*

Feeling Scared

Timed Pair Share Cards

Directions: Cut out cards along the dotted lines. Students share answers to the questions using Timed Pair Share.

1 — Feeling Scared

I feel scared when _______ because _______.

Timed Pair Share

2 — Feeling Scared

Describe a time you were very scared.

Timed Pair Share

3 — Feeling Scared

What would make the scared feeling worse?

Timed Pair Share

4 — Feeling Scared

What makes you feel safe when you are scared?

Timed Pair Share

5 — Feeling Scared

What can you say to express you are scared?

Timed Pair Share

6 — Feeling Scared

Why is it important to tell someone if you are scared?

Timed Pair Share

7 — Feeling Scared

What could you do to comfort someone who was scared?

Timed Pair Share

8 — Feeling Scared

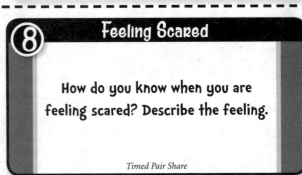

How do you know when you are feeling scared? Describe the feeling.

Timed Pair Share

Feeling Thankful

Three-Step Interview

Purpose

- **To teach students to be thankful for the things they have**
- **To learn more about their teammates and classmates**

Group Size

- Pairs and Teams

Materials

- 1 Feeling Thankful Worksheet per student
- 1 writing utensil per student
- 1 class timer

Preteaching

- Discuss what it means to be thankful.

Activity Overview

In pairs, students interview each other with questions about feeling thankful and then share with teammates what they learned.

Activity Steps

1. The teacher provides the interview topic, *"feeling thankful,"* and sets a time limit.
2. In pairs, Student A interviews Student B using the questions from the Feeling Thankful Worksheet. Student B talks while Student A listens and records.
3. Pairs switch roles. Student B interviews Student A. Student A talks while Student B listens and/or coaches and records.
4. RoundRobin—pairs pair up to form teams of four. Each student takes turns sharing with the team what he or she learned about feeling thankful from the interview.

Structure Alternative
- *Timed Pair Share*

Feeling Thankful

Three-Step Interview Worksheet

Directions: Take turns interviewing your partner. Record your partner's answers and then share answers with your team.

Feeling Thankful Interview Questions

1. What are you most thankful for at home? ______
2. What are you most thankful for at school? ______
3. Who is a friend that you are thankful for? ______
4. What are you most thankful for about yourself? ______
5. Why are you thankful for your teacher? ______
6. How can you show you are thankful for your family? ______
7. How can you show you are thankful for your friends? ______
8. How can you show you are thankful for your teacher? ______
9. How can you show you are thankful for your school? ______
10. What words show you are thankful? ______
11. How can you use your body language to show you are thankful? ______
12. Why is it important to be thankful? ______

Feeling Worried

Talking Chips

Purpose

- **To make sure all students know how to show and express the feeling of being worried in a safe and appropriate way**

Group Size

- Teams

Materials

- 1–2 Talking Chips per student
- 1 class timer

Preteaching

- Teach students it is okay to be worried! When we are worried, we need to make sure we show the feeling in a safe and appropriate way. Using a T-chart, make a list as a class of okay and not okay behaviors when feeling worried.

Activity Overview

Teams have a discussion about feeling worried. Teammates have Talking Chips to make sure everyone contributes to the team discussion.

Activity Steps

1 The teacher passes out one or two chips to each member of the team, provides one discussion question below, or posts them all to facilitate a longer discussion. The teacher sets a timer for an appropriate amount of time, approximately 3–5 minutes.

1. *"I feel worried when _____ because ______."*
2. *"How do you know when you are worried? Where in your body do you notice the worry?"*
3. *"What are some safe and appropriate ways to handle worried feelings?"*
4. *"Who could you talk to about your worried feelings? What would you say?"*
5. *"What are some thoughts you could think that make the worried feelings worse? What are some thoughts that could make the worried feelings better?"*

2 Any student begins the discussion, placing a chip in the center of the table.

3 Any student with a chip continues discussing the feeling worried question, using his or her chip.

4 When all chips are used, teammates each collect their own chips and continue the discussion using their Talking Chips. Teams are not finished until the timer beeps.

Structure Alternatives

- *RoundRobin*
- *Timed Pair Share*

Feeling Worried

Talking Chips

Directions: Cut out the Talking Chips. Give each student one or two chips to play Talking Chips.

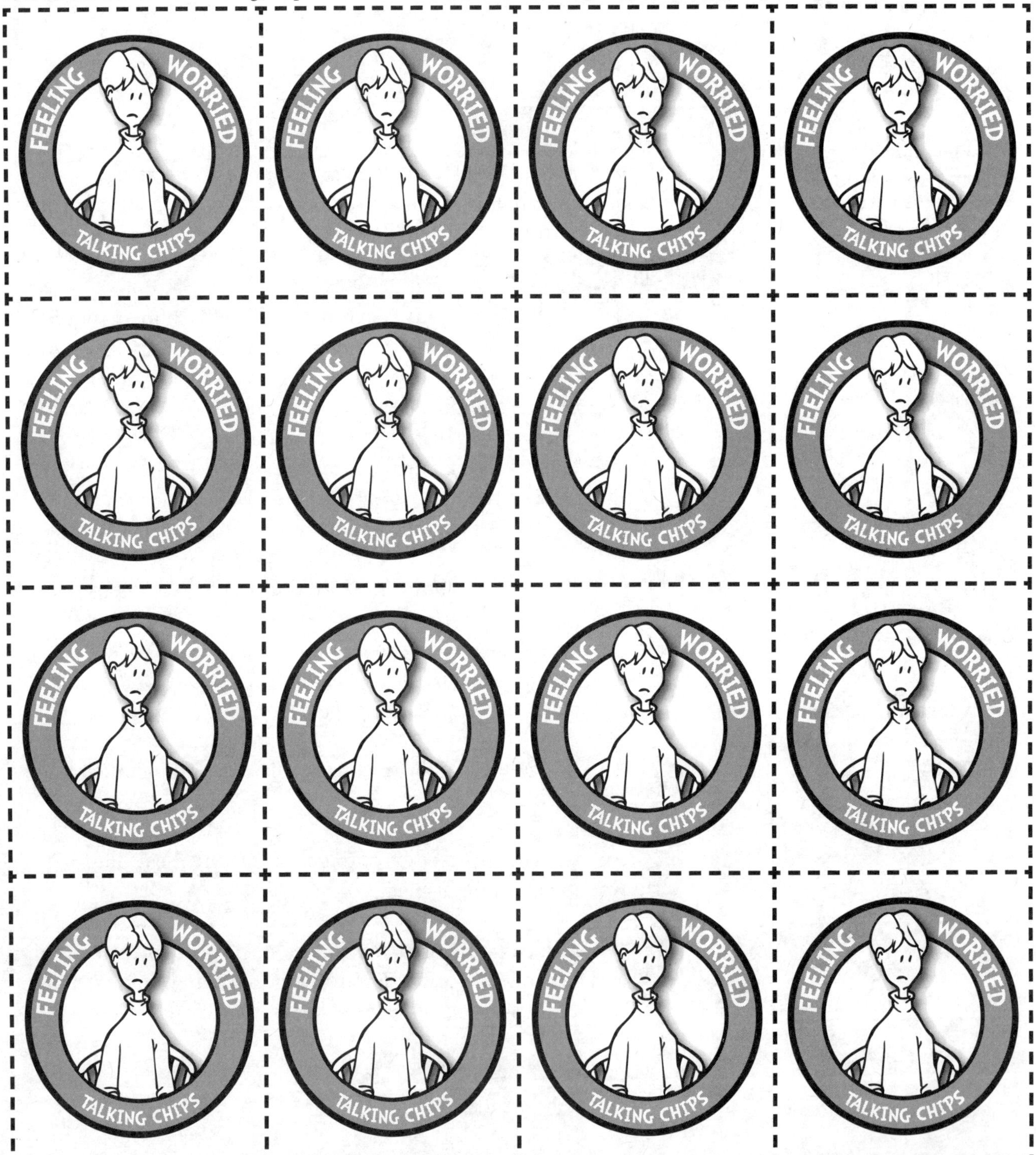

Using I-Messages

Mix-Pair-Share

Purpose

- **To teach students how to put their feelings into words**
- **To enable students to share how they feel**

Group Size

- Pairs

Materials

- 1 set of Using I-Messages cards per class

Preteaching

- Teach the basic format for an I-message: *"I feel ___ when ___."* Or, *"I feel ___ when ____ because _____."* Give several examples.

Activity Overview

The class "mixes" until the teacher calls, "Pair." *The teacher asks students questions. Students respond to a partner using the I-Message format. Students find a new partner to respond to each question.*

Activity Steps

1. The students mix around the room.
2. The teacher calls, *"Pair."*
3. Students pair up with the person closest to them and give a high five. Students who haven't found a partner raise their hands to quickly find each other.
4. The teacher asks a question such as, *"When do you feel disappointed?"*, and gives students Think Time.
5. Students share with their partners using Timed Pair Share. Students use the I-Message format as they respond to the questions.

Structure Alternatives

- *Fan-N-Pick*
- *Numbered Heads Together*
- *Talking Chips*

Using I-Messages

Mix-Pair-Share Cards

Directions: Cut out each card along the dotted lines. In pairs, students take turns responding to the question.

1 Using I-Messages

When do you feel happy? Why?

Mix-Pair-Share

2 Using I-Messages

When do you feel sad? Why?

Mix-Pair-Share

3 Using I-Messages

When do you feel annoyed? Why?

Mix-Pair-Share

4 Using I-Messages

When do you feel mad? Why?

Mix-Pair-Share

5 Using I-Messages

When do you feel calm? Why?

Mix-Pair-Share

6 Using I-Messages

When do you feel proud? Why?

Mix-Pair-Share

7 Using I-Messages

When do you feel disappointed? Why?

Mix-Pair-Share

8 Using I-Messages

When do you feel excited? Why?

Mix-Pair-Share

Character Education

Cheating

Talking Chips

Purpose

- **To make sure all students understand when assignments need to be completed independently and when it is okay to see other students' work**

Group Size

- Teams

Materials

- 1–2 Talking Chips per student
- 1 class timer

Preteaching

- Teach the definition of the word "cheating." As a class, hold a short discussion on your expectations on what work is to be completed independently and what work is okay to be completed together.
- Cheating in school means you take someone else's work as your own. Cheating disregards the rules of honesty.

Activity Overview

Teams discuss cheating. Teammates have Talking Chips to make sure everyone contributes to the team discussion.

Activity Steps

1. The teacher passes out one or two chips to each member of the team, provides one discussion question below, or posts them all to facilitate a longer discussion. The teacher sets a timer for an appropriate amount of time, approximately 3–5 minutes.
   1. *"Sometimes people have the temptation to cheat. What are some reasons why people would decide to cheat?"*
   2. *"What are some reasons why people would decide NOT to cheat?"*
   3. *"Who does cheating hurt? How so?"*
   4. *"What are some examples of the ways people cheat?"*
2. Any student begins the discussion, placing a chip in the center of the table.
3. Any student with a chip continues discussing the cheating question, using his or her chip.
4. When all chips are used, teammates each collect their own chips and continue the discussion using their Talking Chips. Teams are not finished until the timer beeps.

Structure Alternatives

- *RoundRobin*
- *Timed Pair Share*

Cheating

Talking Chips

Directions: Cut out the Talking Chips. Give each student one or two chips to play Talking Chips.

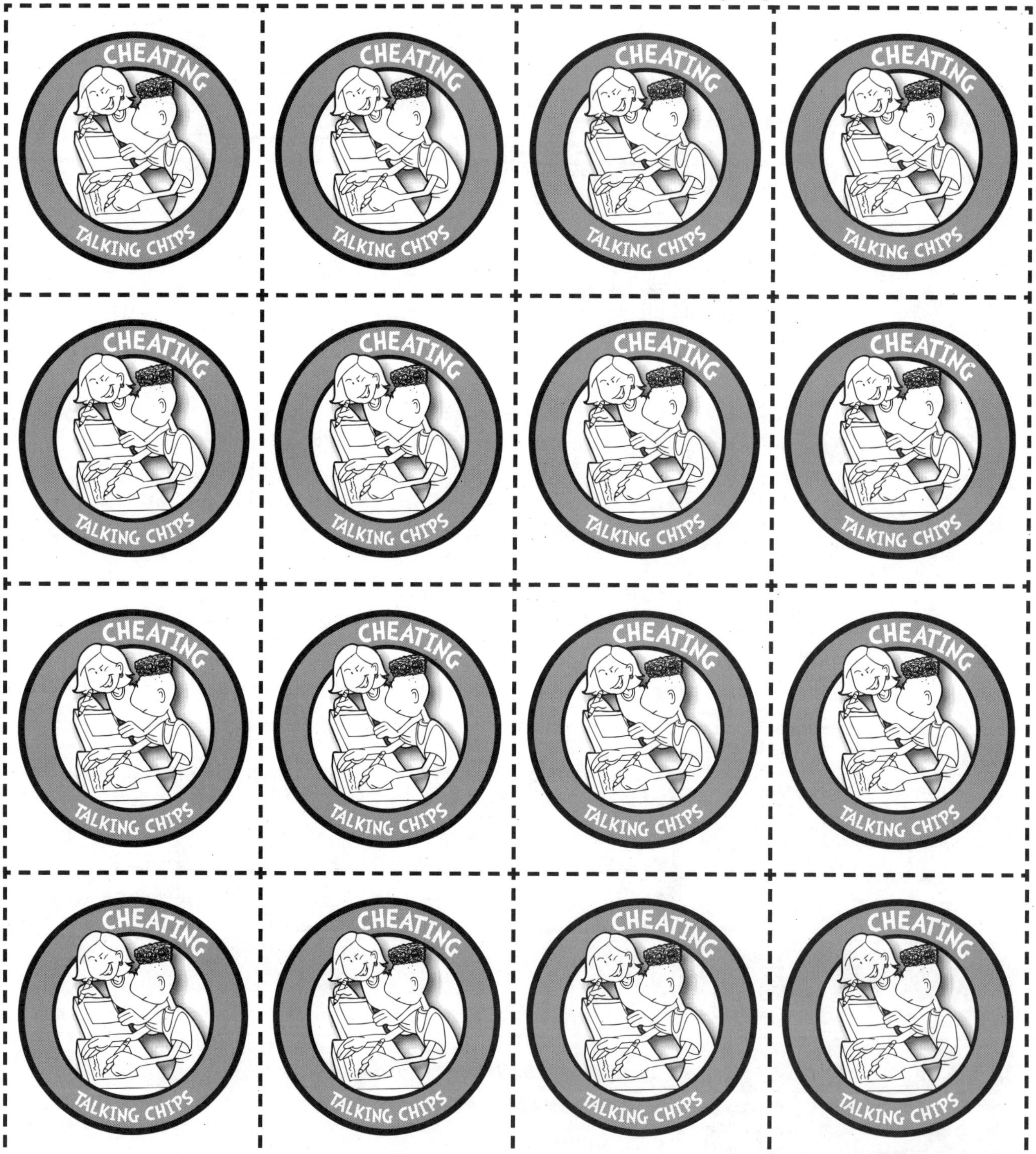

Cooperation

Talking Chips

Purpose

- **To make sure all students understand the importance of cooperation**
- **To increase cooperation in the school**

Group Size

- Teams

Materials

- 1–2 Talking Chips per student
- 1 class timer

Preteaching

- Teach the definition of the word "cooperation." Cooperation is the act of working together for a common purpose. Brainstorm a time when cooperation might be needed in the classroom.

Activity Overview

Teams have a discussion on cooperation. Teammates have Talking Chips to make sure everyone contributes to the team discussion.

Activity Steps

1. The teacher passes out one or two chips to each member of the team, provides one discussion question below, or posts them all to facilitate a longer discussion. The teacher sets a timer for an appropriate amount of time, approximately 3–5 minutes.
   1. *"What type of person do you enjoy working with? Explain why."*
   2. *"What is fun about cooperation?"*
   3. *"What is tough about cooperation?"*
   4. *"Are you an easy person to cooperate with? Why or why not?"*
   5. *"What personal characteristics are important for teamwork?"*
2. Any student begins the discussion, placing a chip in the center of the table.
3. Any student with a chip continues discussing the cooperation question, using his or her chip.
4. When all chips are used, teammates each collect their own chips and continue the discussion using their Talking Chips. Teams are not finished until the timer beeps.

Structure Alternatives

- *RoundRobin*
- *Timed Pair Share*

Cooperation

Talking Chips

Directions: Cut out the Talking Chips. Give each student one or two chips to play Talking Chips.

Honesty

Fan-N-Pick

Purpose

- To teach students that being honest is a part of being responsible and respectful
- To make sure all students understand that there are many situations in life in which individuals have to choose between lying and telling the truth

Group Size

- Teams

Materials

- 1 set of Honesty cards per team
- 1 Fan-N-Pick Mat per team (optional)

Preteaching

- Explain the difference between the truth and a lie. Give several examples of each. Explain that when you tell the truth, it is called being honest.
- Explain the term "exaggeration."
- Explain how honesty is part of responsibility and respect. Give several examples.

Activity Overview

Teammates play a card game to respond to the questions or statements about honesty. Roles rotate with each new question or statement.

Activity Steps

1. Student #1 holds the Honesty cards in a fan and says, *"Pick a card, any card!"*
2. Student #2 picks a card, reads the question or statement aloud, and allows 5 seconds of Think Time.
3. Student #3 answers the question or statement about honesty.
4. Student #4 responds to the answer:
   - For right or wrong answers, student #4 checks and then either praises or tutors.
   - For questions that have no right or wrong answer, Student #4 does not check for correctness, but praises and then paraphrases the thinking that went into the answer.
5. Students rotate roles, one person clockwise for each new round.

Note: A Fan-N-Pick Mat can be placed in the center of the table to lead students through the structure, ensuring everyone keeps actively involved.

Structure Alternatives

- *Mix-Pair-Share*
- *Timed Pair Share*
- *StandUp–HandUp–PairUp*
- *Numbered Heads Together*

Honesty

Fan-N-Pick Cards

Directions: Cut out each card along the dotted lines. Give each team a set of cards to play Fan-N-Pick.

1 Honesty

When have you lied?
Did you regret it? Why?

Fan-N-Pick

2 Honesty

Do you think it is ever okay to lie?
Why or why not?

Fan-N-Pick

3 Honesty

Some people exaggerate the truth. Is this lying? Explain.

Fan-N-Pick

4 Honesty

Give an example of someone who lied and explain how the lie got them into big trouble.

Fan-N-Pick

5 Honesty

If you lie, people don't believe you even when you tell the truth. Do you agree with this statement? Why?

Fan-N-Pick

6 Honesty

When were you lied to?
How did it make you feel?

Fan-N-Pick

7 Honesty

What would happen if everyone told lies all the time?

Fan-N-Pick

8 Honesty

If you lie, who does it hurt?
How?

Fan-N-Pick

Honesty

Fan-N-Pick Blank Template

Directions: Use these blank cards to create your own Fan-N-Pick Honesty cards.

Honesty Fan-N-Pick	Honesty Fan-N-Pick
Honesty Fan-N-Pick	Honesty Fan-N-Pick
Honesty Fan-N-Pick	Honesty Fan-N-Pick
Honesty Fan-N-Pick	Honesty Fan-N-Pick

Honesty

Fan-N-Pick Mat

Directions: Copy and cut out the Fan-N-Pick Mat along the dotted lines. Place the mat in the center of table to play Fan-N-Pick.

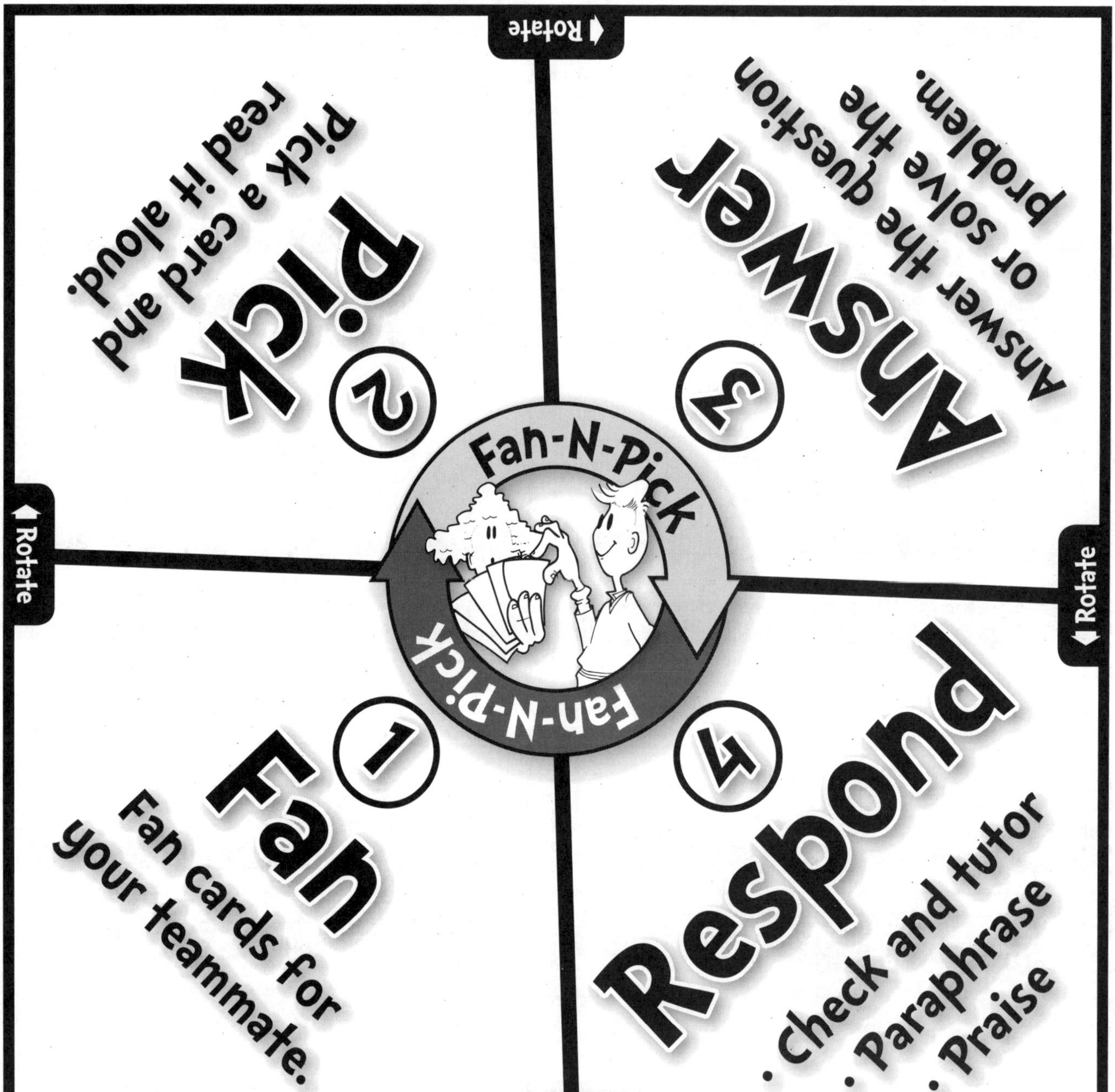

Impulse Control

RallyTable and Pairs Compare

Purpose

- **To teach students about impulse control**

Group Size

- Pairs

Materials

- 1 Impulse Control Worksheet per pair
- 1 writing utensil per student

Preteaching

- Teach students about what an "impulse" is. An impulse is a strong urge or desire to act. People can have impulses to do right or wrong things. For example, someone might have an impulse to help someone in need. Or someone might have the impulse to steal something. We all have impulses that need to be controlled. We need to act on the good impulses and choose to disregard the bad impulses.

Activity Overview

In pairs, students take turns generating ideas about impulse control. Together, students list examples in either the "Impulses to Act On" column or the "Impulses to Disregard" column. Pairs compare their answers with another pair.

Activity Steps

RallyTable:

1. The teacher announces the topic is *"impulse control"* and passes out the Impulse Control Worksheet to each pair. The teacher tells students that they will generate a list of examples of impulses students (or teachers) should act on under the "Impulses to Act On" column, and impulses to disregard under the "Impulses to Disregard" column.
2. The teacher asks students to think about good impulses and bad impulses and provides Think Time.
3. The teacher announces which student will start the list.
4. Students write an idea in one column and the opposite idea in the other. (For example, helping someone is an impulse to act on and stealing is an impulse to disregard.) Students pass the paper back and forth to each other after they have made a contribution. (Students may not pass the paper without making a contribution. They may not make more than one contribution at a time.)
5. The teacher calls time.

Pairs Compare:

6. Pairs pair to RoundRobin their answers. For each answer, the face partner in the other pair adds the answer to that pair's list or checks it off if they already had it.
7. As a team of four, they see if they can come up with additional ideas.

Structure Alternatives

- *Jot Thoughts*
- *Talking Chips*
- *AllRecord RoundRobin*

Impulse Control

RallyTable and Pairs Compare Worksheet

Directions: Take turns listing impulses to act on and impulses to disregard in the appropriate columns.

Impulses to Act on	Impulses to Disregard
Example: Picking up trash **Example:** Giving	**Example:** Throwing trash on the ground **Example:** Stealing

Manners

Talking Chips

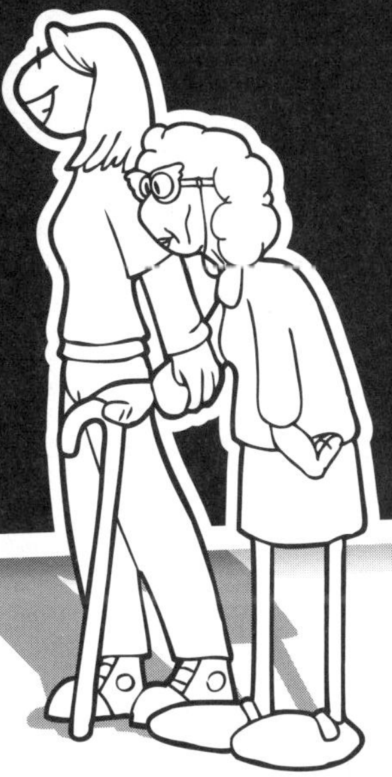

Purpose

- To make sure all students understand the importance of manners
- To increase respect in the school

Group Size

- Teams

Materials

- 1–2 Talking Chips per student
- 1 class timer

Proteaching

- As a class generate two lists:
  - Manners
  - Rude behavior
- Explain how manners are a big part of being respectful.

Activity Overview

Teams have a discussion on manners. Teammates have Talking Chips to make sure everyone contributes to the team discussion.

Activity Steps

1. The teacher passes out one or two chips to each member of the team, provides one discussion question below, or posts them all to facilitate a longer discussion. The teacher sets a timer for an appropriate amount of time, approximately 3–5 minutes.
   1. *"What are some examples of good manners you can use at your school? (Think of the playground, cafeteria, hallway, classroom, etc.)"*
   2. *"Does everyone deserve to be treated politely? Why or why not?"*
   3. *"How do you know what behavior is appropriate for a situation? For example, it is okay to cheer loudly at a basketball game but not in a restaurant?"*
   4. *"What are more examples of behaviors that are allowed in some places but not others?"*

2. Any student begins the discussion, placing a chip in the center of the table.

3. Any student with a chip continues discussing the manners question, using his or her chip.

4. When all chips are used, teammates each collect their own chips and continue the discussion using their Talking Chips. Teams are not finished until the timer beeps.

Structure Alternatives

- *RoundRobin*
- *Timed Pair Share*

Manners

Talking Chips

Directions: Cut out the Talking Chips. Give each student one or two chips to play Talking Chips.

Positive Attitude

Timed Pair Share

Purpose

- **To increase respect and responsibly within our school**

Group Size

- Pairs and Teams

Materials

- 1 set of Positive Attitude cards per class or pair
- 1 class timer

Preteaching

- Teach students how we can have a powerful effect on how we act and how we feel. Give several examples of positive and negative thinking and how it can have an effect on a situation.

Activity Overview

In pairs, students take turns sharing their responses to questions about positive attitude.

Activity Steps

1. The teacher either reads a Positive Attitude card or Partner A draws a card and reads it aloud to his or her partner. The teacher states that each student will have 20 seconds to share, and then provides Think Time for students to think about how they will respond.
2. In pairs, Partner A shares and Partner B listens.
3. Partner B responds with praise.
4. Partners switch roles: Partner B responds to the question, and then Partner A praises Partner B for his or her response.

Structure Alternatives

- *Mix-Pair-Share*
- *Fan-N-Pick*
- *RallyRobin*
- *Talking Chips*

Positive Attitude

Timed Pair Share Cards

Directions: Cut out cards along the dotted lines. Students share answers to the questions using Timed Pair Share.

Positive Attitude

When do you find it easy to have a positive attitude? Why?

Timed Pair Share

Positive Attitude

When is it hard to have a positive attitude? Why?

Timed Pair Share

Positive Attitude

What are some things someone with a positive attitude might say?

Timed Pair Share

Positive Attitude

What are some things someone with a positive attitude might think?

Timed Pair Share

Positive Attitude

What are some things someone with a positive attitude might do?

Timed Pair Share

Positive Attitude

Describe how someone with a positive attitude acts at recess and P.E.

Timed Pair Share

Positive Attitude

Describe how someone with a positive attitude acts in the classroom during learning time.

Timed Pair Share

Positive Attitude

How would someone with a positive attitude approach a challenge? What is a challenge for you at school? Do you have a positive attitude?

Timed Pair Share

Showing Respect

Fact or Fiction

Purpose

- **To teach students to be respectful**

Group Size

- Teams

Materials

- 1 set of Showing Respect cards per team
- 1 "Fact" and 1 "Fiction" response card per student

Preteaching

- Teach the word "respect." Respect means treating people well or treating others the same way you like to be treated. Give several examples of the respect and disrespect. It is a skill that students need to be successful in life. Respect is a personal characteristic that staff members expect students to demonstrate in all areas of the school.
- Teach the words "fact" and "fiction." Practice several easy statements to make sure the class understands how to play.

Activity Overview

Students detect facts that appear false and fictions that appear true about showing respect.

Activity Steps

Teacher Directed

1. The teacher reads a true or false statement from the Showing Respect cards.
2. Each teammate makes his or her best guess by holding up a "Fact" or "Fiction" response card indicating if the statement is fact or fiction.
3. The teacher applauds students who answered correctly.
4. The process is repeated.

Student Directed

1. In teams, one student per team stands and reads the statement on the Showing Respect card.
2. Teammates think and then share their guesses by holding up a "Fact" or "Fiction" response card indicating if the statement is fact or fiction.
3. If correct, the standing student claps for those who are correct.
4. The process is repeated as teammates take turns reading a new card and leading the team through the cards.

Structure Alternative

- *Showdown*

Showing Respect

Fact or Fiction Response Cards

Directions: Cut out each card along the dotted lines. Give each student one "Fact" and one "Fiction" response card to play Fact or Fiction.

Showing Respect

Fact

Fact or Fiction

Showing Respect

Fact

Fact or Fiction

Showing Respect

Fiction

Fact or Fiction

Showing Respect

Fiction

Fact or Fiction

Showing Respect

Fact or Fiction Cards

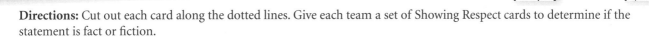

Directions: Cut out each card along the dotted lines. Give each team a set of Showing Respect cards to determine if the statement is fact or fiction.

1 Showing Respect

It is respectful to call someone a rude name.

Fact or Fiction

2 Showing Respect

It is respectful to throw your paper towel into the garbage can.

Fact or Fiction

3 Showing Respect

It is respectful to walk quietly through the hallways.

Fact or Fiction

4 Showing Respect

It is respectful to say, *"You can't play,"* when someone asks to join your game.

Fact or Fiction

5 Showing Respect

It is respectful to use hand sanitizer or wash your hands before using the computer in the lab.

Fact or Fiction

6 Showing Respect

It is respectful to leave garbage at your spot in the cafeteria.

Fact or Fiction

7 Showing Respect

It is respectful to keep your hands to yourself in line.

Fact or Fiction

8 Showing Respect

It is respectful to say thank you when you receive a treat.

Fact or Fiction

Showing Respect

Fact or Fiction Blank Template

Directions: Use these blank cards to create your own Fact or Fiction Showing Respect cards.

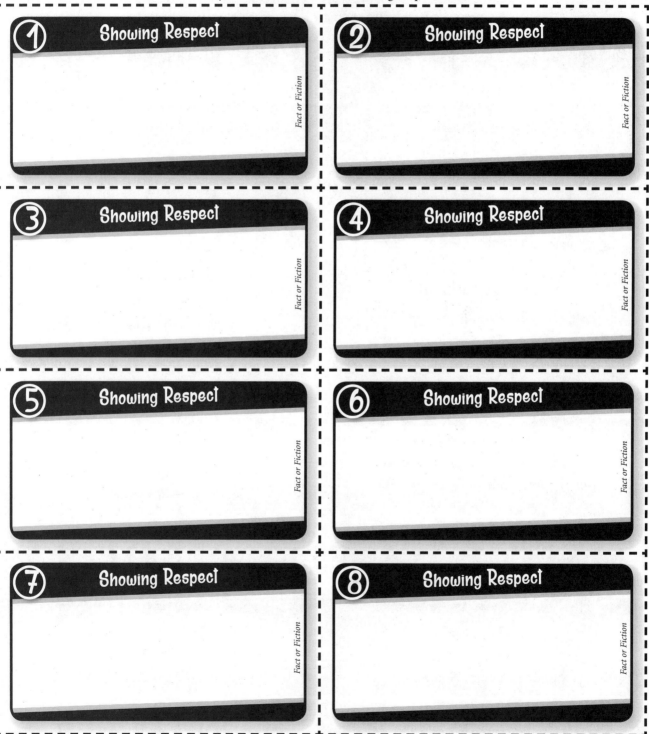

1 Showing Respect

Fact or Fiction

2 Showing Respect

Fact or Fiction

3 Showing Respect

Fact or Fiction

4 Showing Respect

Fact or Fiction

5 Showing Respect

Fact or Fiction

6 Showing Respect

Fact or Fiction

7 Showing Respect

Fact or Fiction

8 Showing Respect

Fact or Fiction

Being Respectful

Rappin' Teams

Purpose

- To build relationships with teammates
- To review what it means to be respectful to others

Group Size

- Teams

Materials

- 1 Being Respectful Key Words Recording Sheet per student
- 1 Being Respectful Rap Rough Draft per team
- 1 Being Respectful Our Final Team Rap worksheet per team
- 1 writing utensil per student
- 1 class timer

Preteaching

- Ensure all students know what respectful means.
- Students should be given examples of when people were respectful.

Activity Overview

Teams develop a rap on being respectful. They perform their raps for another team.

Activity Steps

1. The teacher assigns the rap topic on, *"being respectful."*
2. Teammates use AllRecord RoundRobin to generate and record a list of eight key words. Teammates take turns starting a key word and everyone records it on the Being Respectful Key Words Recording Sheet provided.
3. Teammates use AllRecord RoundRobin again to generate and record three or four rhyming words for each key word on the Being Respectful Key Words Recording Sheet provided.
4. Using the key words, rhyming words, and meter, teammates work together to create lines for their rap using the Rap Rough Draft and then finalize using the Our Final Team Rap worksheet.
5. Teammates practice their rap, deciding roles for each teammate. For examples, which teammates will sing which lines, and which sound effects, clapping, or stomping.
6. Team up—teams perform their rap for another team.

Being Respectful

Rappin' Teams Key Words Recording Sheet

Directions: Students use this sheet to record the key words and rhyming words for each key word.

Key Words That Go with Being Respectful	Rhyming Words
1	1. ______ 2. ______ 3. ______
2	1. ______ 2. ______ 3. ______
3	1. ______ 2. ______ 3. ______
4	1. ______ 2. ______ 3. ______
5	1. ______ 2. ______ 3. ______
6	1. ______ 2. ______ 3. ______
7	1. ______ 2. ______ 3. ______
8	1. ______ 2. ______ 3. ______

Being Respectful

Rappin' Teams Rap Rough Draft

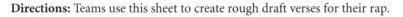

Directions: Teams use this sheet to create rough draft verses for their rap.

Team Rap Rough Draft

Rap Name ______________________________

★ Key word: ________________

Rap verse using the key word and rhyming word(s): ________________

____

____

____

★ Key word: ________________

Rap verse using the key word and rhyming word(s): ________________

____

____

____

★ Key word: ________________

Rap verse using the key word and rhyming word(s): ________________

____

____

____

★ Key word: ________________

Rap verse using the key word and rhyming word(s): ________________

____

____

____

★ Key word: ________________

Rap verse using the key word and rhyming word(s): ________________

____

____

____

Being Respectful

Rappin' Teams Our Final Team Rap

Directions: Teams use this worksheet to finalize and record their rap. When done writing their rap, practice it as a team and prepare to perform it.

Team Rap Final Draft

Rap Name ______________________________

Respect

Talking Chips

Purpose

- To make sure all students understand respect
- To increase respectful behavior in the school

Group Size

- Teams

Materials

- 1–2 Talking Chips per student
- 1 class timer

Preteaching

- Teach the definition of the word "respect." Respect means treating people well or treating others the same way you like to be treated.
- Give examples of respectful behavior.

Activity Overview

Teams have a discussion on respect. Teammates have Talking Chips to make sure everyone contributes to the team discussion.

Activity Steps

1. The teacher passes out one or two chips to each member of the team, provides one discussion question below, or posts them all to facilitate a longer discussion. The teacher sets a timer for an appropriate amount of time, approximately 3–5 minutes.
    1. *"Why is respect so important?"*
    2. *"Who shows you respect? How do they treat you?"*
    3. *"Who is it easy for you to respect? Who is it difficult for you to respect? Explain."*
    4. *"What are some examples of ways you can respect your teacher and classmates? Be specific."*
2. Any student begins the discussion, placing a chip in the center of the table.
3. Any student with a chip continues discussing the respect question, using his or her chip.
4. When all chips are used, teammates each collect their own chips and continue the discussion using their Talking Chips. Teams are not finished until the timer beeps.

Structure Alternatives

- *RoundRobin*
- *Timed Pair Share*

Respect

Talking Chips

Directions: Cut out the Talking Chips. Give each student one or two chips to play Talking Chips.

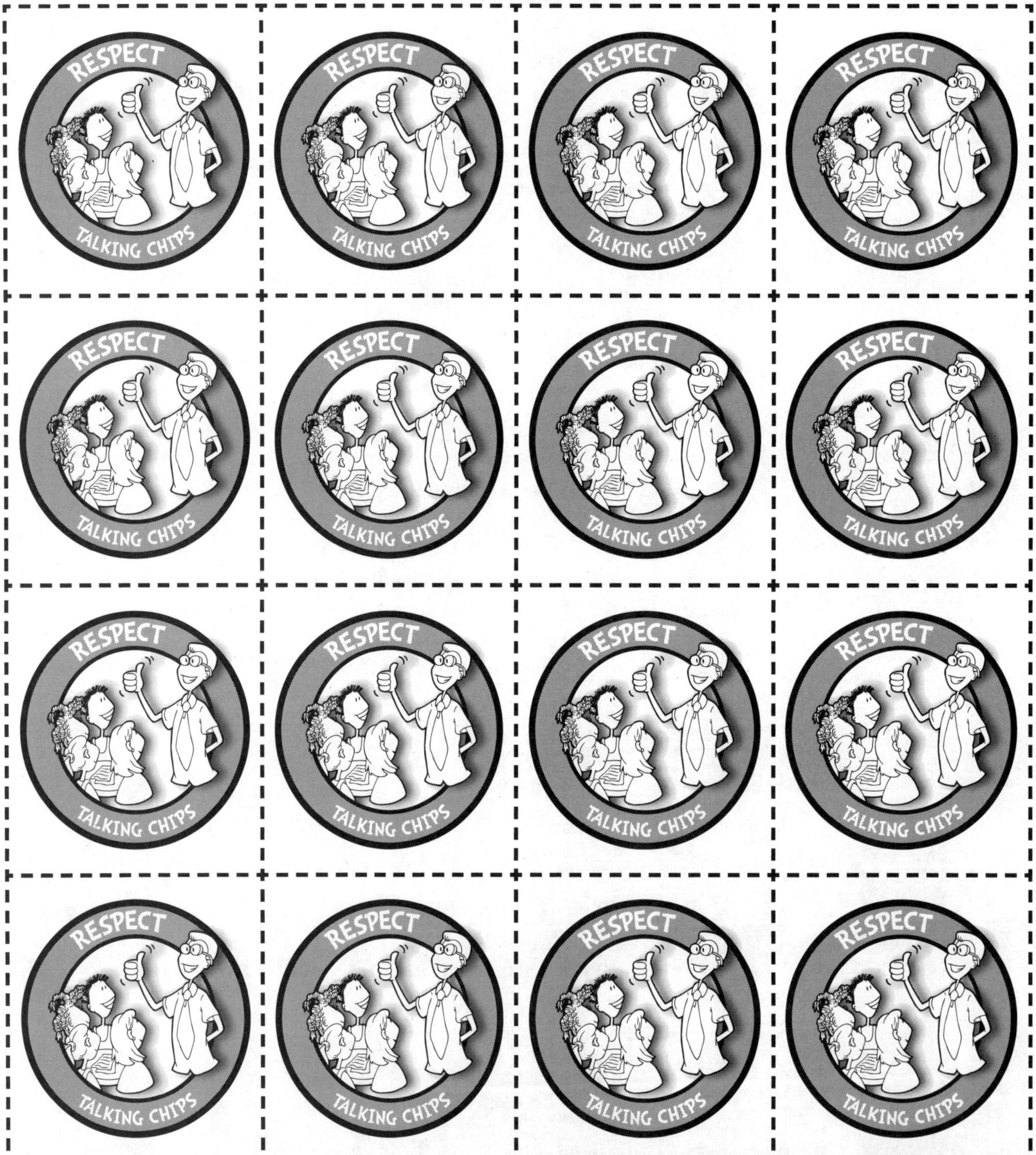

Respect

Think-Write-RoundRobin

Purpose

- **To teach students that being respectful is a skill they need to know to be successful in life**
- **To teach students that respect is a characteristic that staff members expect students to demonstrate in all areas of the school**

Group Size

- Teams

Materials

- 1 sheet of paper per student
- 1 writing utensil per student

Preteaching

- Teach the word "respect." Respect means treating people well or treating others the same way you like to be treated. Give several examples of respect and disrespect.

Activity Overview

Students think and write about respect. Then, they share their thoughts with teammates.

Activity Steps

1. The teacher asks a thinking question about respect. Use one of these questions or come up with your own.
    1. *"What does it mean to treat someone with respect? What things do you do? What things do you say?"*
    2. *"If someone doesn't treat you with respect, would you still treat them with respect? Why or why not?"*
    3. *"What would happen if no one respected anyone else?"*
    4. *"Who is someone that is very respectful? How do they act?"*
    5. *"What is self-respect? How do you show yourself respect?"*
    6. *"Do you consider yourself a respectful person? Why or why not?"*
    7. *"Can you respect someone and not like them? Explain!"*
    8. *"Is aggression ever a good way to gain respect? Why or why not?"*
2. The teacher provides students Think Time to think about their response.
3. Students independently write their responses to the question on a sheet of paper.
4. Students share their written responses with their teammates using RoundRobin, each taking a turn.

Structure Alternatives

- *Jot Thoughts*
- *Talking Chips*
- *RoundRobin*

Responsibility

Mix-Pair-Share

Purpose

- **To teach students to be responsible**

Group Size

- Pairs

Materials

- 1 set of Responsibility cards per class

Preteaching

- Teach the word "responsible." Responsible means to do what you need to do the first time. Give several examples of what it means to be responsible. It is a skill that students need to be successful in life. Responsibility is a characteristic that staff members expect students to demonstrate in all areas of the school.

Activity Overview

The class "mixes" until the teacher calls, "Pair." *The teacher asks students questions about responsibility. Students share with their partner and then find a new partner to discuss or answer the teacher's question about responsibility.*

Activity Steps

1. The students mix around the room.
2. The teacher calls, *"Pair."*
3. Students pair up with the person closest to them and give a high five. Students who haven't found a partner raise their hands to quickly find each other.
4. The teacher asks a question such as, "*What are responsible things to do when you own a pet?*", and gives students Think Time.
5. Students share with their partners using Timed Pair Share.

Structure Alternatives

- *Fan-N-Pick*
- *Numbered Heads Together*
- *Talking Chips*

Responsibility

Mix-Pair-Share Cards

Directions: Cut out each card along the dotted lines. In pairs, students take turns responding to the question or statement.

1 Responsibility

What have the adults in your life told you about being responsible?

Mix-Pair-Share

2 Responsibility

What are some examples of what can happen if you are responsible?

Mix-Pair-Share

3 Responsibility

What are some examples of what can happen if you are not responsible?

Mix-Pair-Share

4 Responsibility

Share about a time when you were very responsible. What happened because you were?

Mix-Pair-Share

5 Responsibility

Share about a time when you were not very responsible. What happened because of this?

Mix-Pair-Share

6 Responsibility

Name two things a student could do to be responsible while getting ready to leave school.

Mix-Pair-Share

7 Responsibility

Name two things a student could do to be responsible while getting ready for school.

Mix-Pair-Share

8 Responsibility

Name one thing a student could do to be responsible about homework.

Mix-Pair-Share

Responsibility

Think-Write-RoundRobin

Purpose

- To teach students that being responsible is a skill they need to know to be successful in life
- To teach students that responsibility is a characteristic that staff members expect students to demonstrate in all areas of the school

Group Size

- Teams

Materials

- 1 sheet of paper per student
- 1 writing utensil per student

Preteaching

- Teach the word "responsible." Responsible means to do what you need to do the first time. Give several examples of what it means to be responsible.
- Go over the cards as a class.

Activity Overview

Students think and write about responsibility. Then, they share their thoughts with teammates.

Activity Steps

1. The teacher ask a thinking question about responsibility. Use one of these questions or come up with your own.
    1. *"What does it mean to be responsible?"*
    2. *"What is a responsible behavior that a student would be doing in the classroom?"*
    3. *"Name one responsibility you have at home."*
    4. *"Name one responsibility you have at school."*
    5. *"Give at least two possible things responsible people might say after making a mistake."*
    6. *"Name three things a student could do to be responsible in the cafeteria."*
    7. *"Name two things a student could do to be responsible on the playground."*
    8. *"Name two things a student could do to be responsible in the bathroom."*
    9. *"Name three things a student could do to be responsible in the hallway."*
2. The teacher provides students Think Time to think about their response.
3. Students independently write their responses to the question on a sheet of paper.
4. Students share their written responses with their teammates using RoundRobin, each taking a turn.

Structure Alternatives

- *Jot Thoughts*
- *Talking Chips*
- *RoundRobin*

Responsibility

Talking Chips

Purpose

- To make sure all students understand what responsibility means and looks like
- To increase responsibility in the school

Group Size

- Teams

Materials

- 1–2 Talking Chips per student
- 1 class timer

Preteaching

- Teach the definition of the word "responsibility." Responsibility means you do something you are expected to do willingly.
- Give examples of responsible behavior.

Activity Overview

Teams have a discussion on responsibility. Teammates have Talking Chips to make sure everyone contributes to the team discussion.

Activity Steps

1. The teacher passes out one or two chips to each member of the team, provides one discussion question below, or posts them all to facilitate a longer discussion. The teacher sets a timer for an appropriate amount of time, approximately 3–5 minutes.
    1. *"What responsibilities do you have in this classroom/school?"*
    2. *"What are the consequences if we are not responsible?"*
    3. *"What responsibilities are easy for you to manage?"*
    4. *"What responsibilities are tough for you to manage?"*
    5. *"What could you do to become more responsible?"*
2. Any student begins the discussion, placing a chip in the center of the table.
3. Any student with a chip continues discussing the responsibility question, using his or her chip.
4. When all chips are used, teammates each collect their own chips and continue the discussion using their Talking Chips. Teams are not finished until the timer beeps.

Structure Alternatives

- *RoundRobin*
- *Timed Pair Share*

Responsibility

Talking Chips

Directions: Cut out the Talking Chips. Give each student one or two chips to play Talking Chips.

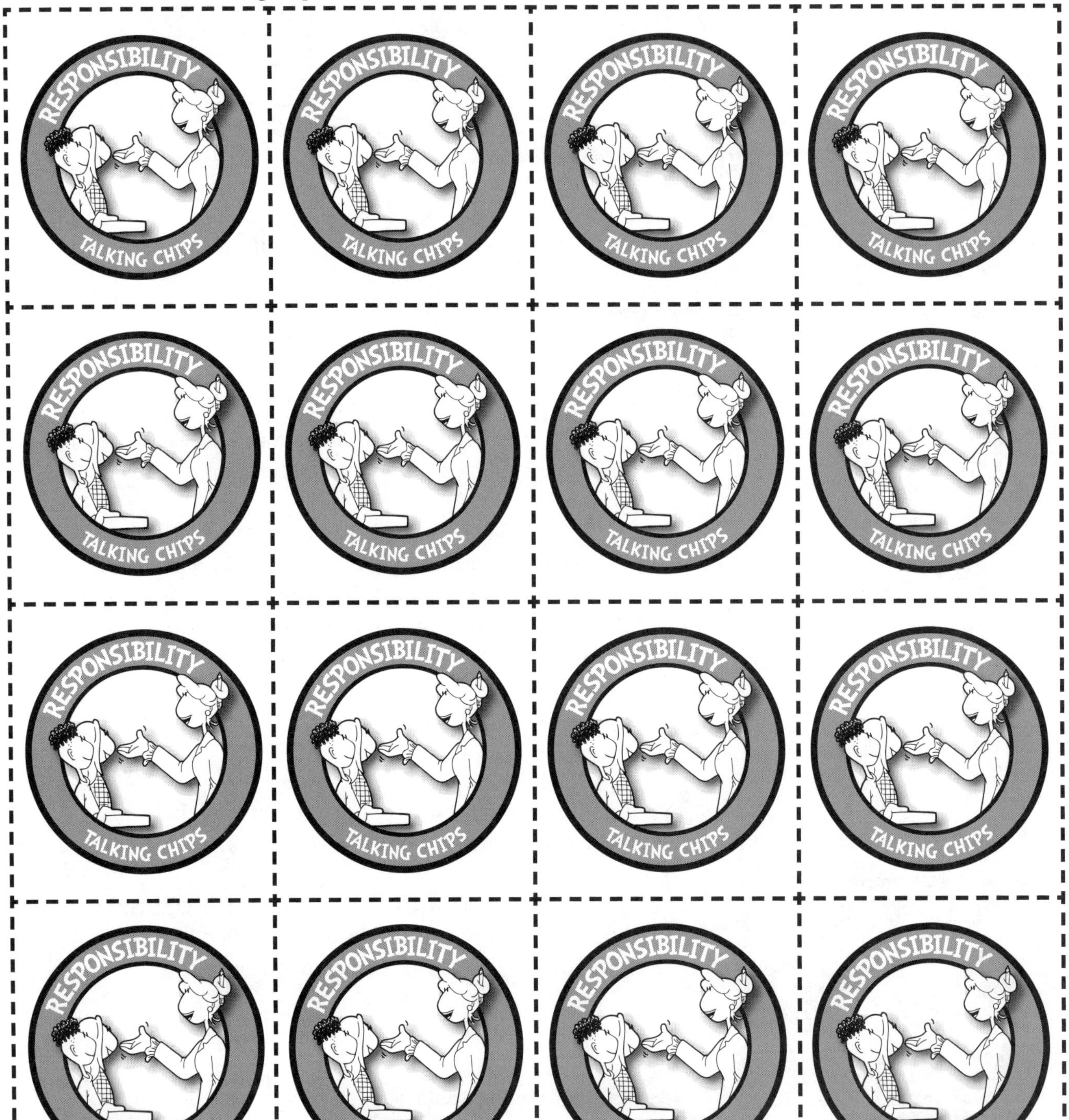

Stealing

Talking Chips

Purpose

- **To make sure all students understand that stealing is against school rules and disrespectful**

Group Size

- Teams

Materials

- 1–2 Talking Chips per student
- 1 class timer

Preteaching

- Explain what it means to "steal" (taking something that doesn't belong to you without permission).
- Hold a class discussion and review the rules of the school and laws of society about stealing.

Activity Overview

Teams have a discussion on stealing. Teammates have Talking Chips to make sure everyone contributes to the team discussion.

Activity Steps

1. The teacher passes out one or two chips to each member of the team, provides one discussion question below, or posts them all to facilitate a longer discussion. The teacher sets a timer for an appropriate amount of time, approximately 3–5 minutes.
   1. *"If someone has stolen, what should they do?"*
   2. *"Why do you think people steal?"*
   3. *"Is it ever okay to steal?"*
   4. *"How can you stop yourself from stealing if you have that temptation?"*
2. Any student begins the discussion, placing a chip in the center of the table.
3. Any student with a chip continues discussing the stealing question, using his or her chip.
4. When all chips are used, teammates each collect their own chips and continue the discussion using their Talking Chips. Teams are not finished until the timer beeps.

Structure Alternatives

- *RoundRobin*
- *Timed Pair Share*

Stealing

Talking Chips

Directions: Cut out the Talking Chips. Give each student one or two chips to play Talking Chips.

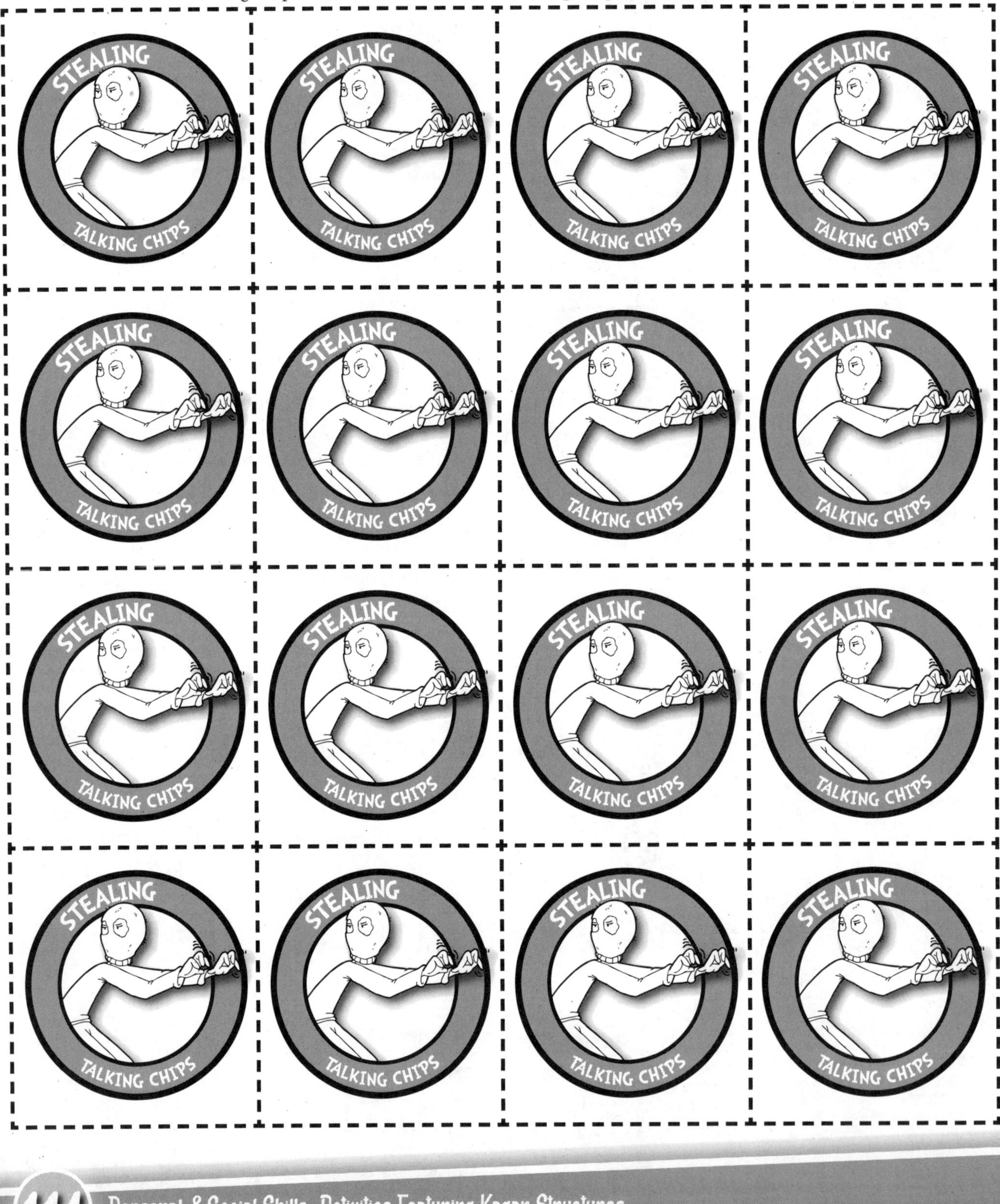

Stealing

Think-Write-RoundRobin

Purpose

- **To teach how stealing is wrong**

Group Size

- Teams

Materials

- 1 piece of paper per student
- 1 writing utensil per student

Preteaching

- Explain what it means to "steal" (taking something that doesn't belong to you without permission).

Activity Overview

Students think and write about stealing. Then, they share their thoughts with teammates.

Activity Steps

1. The teacher ask a thinking question about stealing. Use one of these questions or come up with your own.
    1. *"Why is stealing wrong?"*
    2. *"Do you think taking a pencil that isn't yours is stealing?"*
    3. *"Has anyone ever stolen something of yours? How did you feel?"*
    4. *"If you stole a dime from someone would you be embarrassed to return it?"*
    5. *"What would you do if you saw someone in your class stealing from a classmate?"*
2. The teacher provides students Think Time to think about their response.
3. Students independently write their responses to the question on a sheet of paper.
4. Students share their written responses with their teammates using RoundRobin, each taking a turn.

Structure Alternatives

- *Jot Thoughts*
- *Talking Chips*
- *RoundRobin*

Answer Key

Personal & Social Skills
Answer Key

Section 1: Social Skills Development

• Activities 1–6

• Answers will vary

• Activity 7: Getting Along

• *Showdown (pp. 37–38)*

• **Page 37**

1. Smaller
2. Smaller
3. Bigger
4. Bigger
5. Smaller
6. Smaller
7. Smaller
8. Bigger
9. Bigger
10. Smaller

• **Page 38**

11. Smaller
12. Bigger
13. Smaller
14. Bigger
15. Bigger
16. Smaller
17. Smaller
18. Bigger
19. Smaller
20. Smaller

• Activities 8–10

• Answers will vary

• Activity 11: Hands and Feet to Self

• *Showdown (pp. 49–50)*

• **Page 49**

1. Not OK!
2. OK!
3. OK!
4. OK!
5. Not OK!
6. Not OK!
7. Not OK!
8. OK!
9. OK!
10. Not OK!

• **Page 50**

11. OK!
12. OK!
13. OK!
14. OK!
15. Not OK!
16. Not OK!
17. OK!
18. OK!
19. Not OK!
20. Not OK!

• Activity 12

• Answers will vary

Section 2: Emotional Intelligence

• Activities 13–23

• Answers will vary

Personal & Social Skills
Answer Key

Section 3: Character Education

• Activities 24–29

- Answers will vary

• Activity 30: Showing Respect

- ***Fact or Fiction (p. 97)***

1. Fiction	2. Fact
3. Fact	4. Fiction
5. Fact	6. Fiction
7. Fact	8. Fact

• Activities 31–38

- Answers will vary

Notes

Notes

Personal & Social Skills

Notes

Personal & Social Skills

Notes

Personal & Social Skills

Notes

Personal & Social Skills

Notes

Personal & Social Skills

Notes

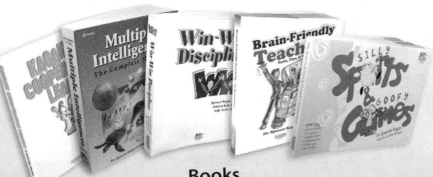